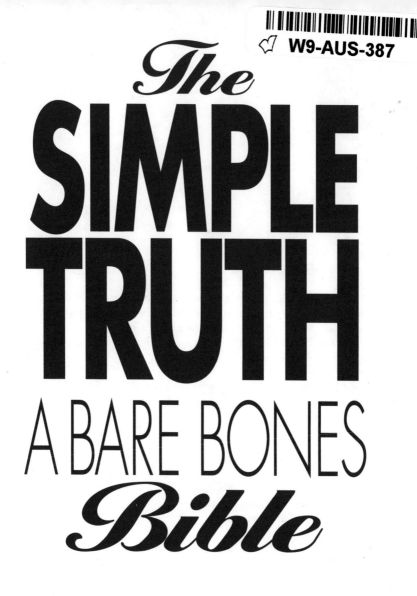

The SIMPLE TRUTH

A BARE BONES *Bible*

WALTER WANGERIN JR.

Group

Loveland, Colorado

The Simple Truth: A Bare Bones Bible
Copyright © 1996 Nickel Press

Published by special arrangement with Nickel Press, Indianapolis, Indiana. *The Simple Truth: A Bare Bones Bible* was adapted from an earlier work written by Walter Wangerin Jr.

Credits
Compiler: Paul Woods
Editor: Bob Buller
Managing Editor: Michael D. Warden
Chief Creative Officer: Joani Schultz
Copy Editor: Janis Sampson
Art Director: Lisa Chandler
Cover Art Director: Helen Lannis
Computer Graphic Artist: Ray Tollison
Cover Designer: Paetzold Design
Production Manager: Gingar Kunkel

ISBN 1-55945-630-2 (Hardcover)
ISBN 1-55945-631-0 (Softcover)

10 9 8 7 6 5 4 3 2 1   05 04 03 02 01 00 99 98 97 96
Printed in the United States of America.

One Story

Through and through the many books of the Bible there weaves a single, living thread. Neither complete nor whole in any one book, this thread is the story of the acts of God among and for his people.

So the Bible is not many little stories with little or no connection with each other; it is one story that extends from the first page to the last. Each individual part rests on all the previous parts and supports the parts to come. A wise way to read this story, then, would be to begin at the beginning; to wonder and grow throughout, as the story speaks wonders and grows branch from vine and blossom from branch; and to neglect no part of it.

Since the purpose of this book is to ravel from the Bible the thread of holy history and to present it lean, clean, and sequential, certain portions of Scripture shall not be found here.

Neither do I pretend to have made a translation of the Bible.

Nor, if one significant event is told several times over in Scripture, do I repeat that event more than once. Rather I've gathered its various tellings into a single scene.

Details I have added, here and there, to liven the narrative as narrative. I meant in reverence to produce a work of art, a song acceptable to God and pleasing to humans. These details have been derived from the geography and the times in which the Bible stories occurred and have been written in harmony with the holiness of Scripture.

All of this is to say that my small offering does not propose to be the Bible in your home or in your heart. Rather, like the stained-glass windows of a cathedral, it is happy to reflect in color, light, and simple art, in joy and faithful worship, the holy history recorded in the Bible.

It is my hope that the stories that follow will give you a taste of God's Word and leave you hungering for more. With that in mind, I have added, at the end of this book, a "For Further Reading" section that lists where each story may be found in a traditional Bible. I encourage you to refer to this section often and to savor the full riches of each story in its original biblical form.

To these words, to all the words and work within this book, I add my honest prayer: To God alone be the glory!

Walter Wangerin Jr.

God Creates the World

In the beginning God created the heavens and the earth. The earth had no shape; there was only emptiness, darkness, and the terrible deep. But God's Spirit was moving over the waters . . .

Then God spoke. "Let there be light!" he commanded. And there was light, and it was good. He separated the light from the darkness so that there was day and night. That was the first day.

Again God spoke: "Let there be a vast roof in the middle of the waters to separate the waters below from the waters above!" And it was just as God had said. He called this roof heaven. That was the second day.

God said, "Let the waters under the heavens come together in a single place! Let dry land appear!" And it was so. He called the dry land earth; he called the gathered waters seas. "Let the earth grow things," he said, "plants, trees, and seeds in each that more and more might grow!" It happened just as God had said, and it was good. That was the third day.

God said, "Let there be lights in the heavens to separate day from night! They will be for telling time and for giving light to the earth!" So God made a great light over the day, a little light over the night, and stars beyond counting. That was the fourth day.

God said, "Let the waters swarm with living creatures! Let birds fly in the sky!" And the waters teemed with life, and the skies were filled with the sight and the sounds of birds! "Good!" said God. "Now bear your young until the skies and the seas burst with life!" That was the fifth day.

On the sixth day God made the beasts, the four-footed and the furry and those covered with scales and those with skin, the cattle and all that crawl. Then on that same sixth day of creation, the Lord God did something with a most particular care: He made humans.

The dust of the earth the Lord God molded until its shape was that of a man. Then he took it; then he himself breathed life into it. Into this dust he breathed the breath of life—and the man became a living being!

A human—in the image of God!

Unto this man the Lord God spoke. "Listen," he said. "Every living thing that I have made I give to you: everything, that you might rule over it; everything, that you might care for it. Everything."

Then God planted a pleasant garden in Eden. There were trees and fruit and rivers in wonderful abundance, and in the center of the garden was the tree of the knowledge of good and evil. This garden, too, was for humankind.

"You will tend it," the Lord God said as he put the man there. "You will till my garden and rejoice in it. But of the tree that is in the center of it—the tree of the knowledge of good and evil—of that tree you must not eat lest you die."

Then God gazed at the man in the garden and thought, "No—man is alone, and he should not be. I will make a mate perfectly fit for him."

So God brought the animals to the man. One by one the man named them, but among the animals none was perfect for him.

So God said "hush" to the man and put him to sleep. He took a rib out of the man and fashioned it into a woman. And the woman was perfectly right for the man!

"This one! This one! This one, at last!" said the man. "Bone of my bones and flesh of my flesh! Did she come from man? Then I will call her woman." And all the while these two lived in Eden, they were naked but never ashamed.

Everything that the Lord God had made was very good, so on the seventh day he rested.

Adam and Eve Disobey God

More than any other creature that God had made, the snake was sly, the snake was clever.

One day he talked with the woman, Eve. "Did God really say," he asked, "that you should not eat from any tree in Eden?"

"Oh, no!" she said. "We can eat of all the trees—except for the one in the middle. If we so much as touch that tree, we will die."

"Die?" asked the snake. "Did God say 'die'? You won't die. Why, God knows that if you eat of it you will become like him, knowing good and evil together. Not death, woman, but wisdom is in the eating!"

Eve looked at the tree. It was lovely, and its fruit looked sweet. And eating, mere eating, might make her wise . . .

She plucked a piece of fruit. She ate it. She gave some to Adam, her husband, and he ate too. They stared at each other.

They stared, and suddenly they grew hot with shame—

because now their nakedness seemed a vile and shameful thing.

Quickly, quickly they snatched leaves, sewed them together, and covered themselves. But this was not enough. So when they heard the footsteps of the Lord God, the Almighty Creator, walking through his garden, they covered themselves from foot to forehead in the brush. They hid from him, and they shook.

"Adam! Where are you?" the Lord God called.

"Hiding," said Adam, his face turned to the dust.

"Why are you hiding?" asked God.

"I am frightened," said Adam.

"And why," said the Lord, "are you frightened?"

"I—I am," the poor man whimpered, "I am naked."

"So!" The Lord God spoke low and slow to the man he had made. "Who told you that you were naked? Adam, Adam, you ate of the tree!"

But Adam leaped to defend himself. "The woman!" he cried. "The woman gave the fruit to me!"

"Eve?" said the Lord. "You?"

"Me?" she cried. Then she, too, made an excuse. "No! The snake! Find the snake, and you'll find the one who tricked me into eating!"

The man, the woman, the snake—the Lord God had made all three. Now this is what he said to them:

"Snake, get down on your belly, low, low down until the end of time. Get down and crawl! Such is my curse on you for what you have done. Your offspring and the children of this woman will be enemies, but hers shall crush yours.

"Eve, when you bear those children, the labor and the bearing will be difficult for you, and your husband shall rule over you.

"Adam, Adam—because you have disobeyed my word, this very dirt is cursed. Weeds, thorns, briars—the dirt shall bring forth a tangled patch, and you shall suffer sweat to work it. But you shall work the dirt until the day you go back into it. Dust you are, Adam, and to dust you will return."

Then the Lord God sent them out of the garden. On the east side of Eden, he set guards and a flaming sword, flashing like lightning to bar the way.

The Great Flood

Ages and ages went by. Men and women had children, and their children had children. Eventually people spread throughout the earth.

But they were a wicked lot, these people. Wherever the Lord God looked, he saw, to his sorrow, their violence. People became so bad that God grew sorry he had ever made them. So God said, "I shall rid the earth of their kind. I shall be done with them."

But there was one good man among the many. There was Noah, righteous and upright. To Noah alone the Lord spoke, "I have determined to destroy this cruel population and all life with it because it has made the whole earth sick. But you, Noah—you. Listen to what I say. Build an ark. Build it as I shall describe it. Get animals, two and two..."

Noah listened, and Noah obeyed.

Out of cypress wood he built his boat with three decks and a roof: a big boat 450 feet long, 75 feet wide, and 45 feet high. He waterproofed the whole with tar, all as the Lord had described.

Then, at God's command, he drove into his ark the animals, every kind of beast there was, a male and female at least of every kind. Finally he sent his sons—Shem, Ham, and Japheth—their wives, and his own wife into the ark. Noah himself entered last, and then God shut the door.

Seven days they waited inside the ark, eight people and all these animals.

Suddenly the storm hit. The windows of heaven opened up, and the rain came down hard—hard and heavy. The ground cracked, and the waters from the deep spouted up in shooting fountains. Water covered the whole face of the earth. The ark began to float. More and more the mighty water swelled until the valleys were filled, the hills disappeared, and the mountains themselves sank out of sight. Forty days and forty nights the hard rain came—and everything and everyone who lived on dry land, every living thing that needed breath in its nostrils to live, died. Only Noah was left, and those who were with him, safe inside the ark.

The rain stopped, but the vast water lasted on the earth 150 days.

In the driving storm, in the lasting flood, God did not forget Noah. He remembered the ark, a chip on the surface of the waters. So he caused a wind to blow, and the wind began to dry the earth.

As the water went down, mountains slowly rose from the ocean, and some of them caught the ark. It came to rest on the peaks of the mountains of Ararat. But still Noah could not go out; his mountaintop was nothing but a tiny island. Still the water went down. After forty days Noah freed a dove into the skies. She flew in search of a place to perch, but she found only water. She came back. Seven days later he let her fly again. Again she returned to him, but this time she bore in her beak an olive twig!

The water went down and down. One week later Noah released his dove for the final time. She flew away and never came back again. The land was ready for life once more.

"Go forth, Noah—you, your family, and all the creatures with you," the Lord God said unto him. "Go forth, populate the earth, fill it with the living, and hear me: I am done with such destruction. I will do this thing no more. Never again shall water be so dangerous that it covers the whole of the earth. No more. If, when it rains again, you are afraid that the rain shall become a flood like this one, look up. I shall place in the sky a rainbow, a sign of my promise. See that rainbow, and know that this is the last of such terrible floods. Go forth to the land, Noah. Go forth and live."

Over the ages, people did go forth on the earth. And though they became many, they all spoke the same language. In the land of Shinar, they decided to build a city with a tower in the middle—a tower so tall that its top would reach heaven. They would make a name for themselves. But God was not pleased with their arrogant plans, so he made them all speak different languages. Since people could no longer understand each other, they scattered. Their city bore the name of Babel—"confusion." The tower was never finished. Neither was God's love for humans nor God's story.

God Creates a People

Thus begins the long, wonderful story of a family. Abram was the father; he, his son Isaac, Isaac's son Jacob, and Jacob's twelve sons were the grandfathers of this family. After them came many generations. Yet always, no matter how many people were born, they remained one family: Israel.

It was a most special family and, for one particular reason, a unique nation. The reason: God himself chose these people to be his own.

It all began with a command and a promise.

"Abram, rise up," the Lord God said unto him. "This is your country. Leave it. These are your relatives, and this your father's house. Leave them. Go to a land that you know not yet, but which I will show you." That was the command.

The promise was as much a surprise. "Abram, I shall make you a father, a grandfather, and a great-grandfather. Your children shall multiply until they are a family in the thousands. I shall bless you so that you shall be a blessing. Those who bless you, I will bless; and I will curse the one who curses you. In you, Abram, shall all of the families of the earth be blessed!"

Abram heard the words of God. Quietly he gathered his possessions. He told Sarai, his wife, that he knew not where they were going, yet they must be gone. He invited his nephew Lot to come along, and then they left.

To the west and the south they traveled hundreds of miles—stopping, moving, stopping, and moving again—until they came to the land of Canaan, to a place called Shechem.

Here the Lord God made Abram another spectacular promise.

"Look west, Abram," he said, "as far as you can see. Look east. Now, to the north and to the south, look! One day all of this land shall belong to the children of your children. I will give it to them!" So Abram built an altar in that place in Canaan and worshiped the Lord his God.

Abram was seventy-five years old when he left Haran to wander through the strange land of Canaan. Soon he was eighty-five, then ninety, and then an old, old man of a hundred long years. In all that time, Sarai, herself grown ninety years old, did not bear him a son.

But God had promised him a son and a family numbering in the thousands, and God kept repeating that promise so Abram could not forget it.

Eventually the Lord God did more than merely speak his promise to Abram. He ensured it. He signed and sealed it, as it were. He entered into a covenant with Abram.

One night after Abram had prepared animal sacrifices, God came to him as he slept. "Is your name Abram?" God asked. "It shall be Abram no more, but Abraham, for you shall be the father of many nations. And no more shall your wife's name be Sarai, but Sarah: 'princess' of a people.

"Abraham, I am making my covenant with you and with all your descendants. Hereafter, you and all the sons of your family shall bear the mark of my covenant on your bodies. From this time forward and forever, you and your sons shall be circumcised."

Suddenly there appeared out of the dreadful darkness a smoking fire pot and a flaming torch. These glowing symbols of the presence of Almighty God assured Abraham that the promise would most certainly be kept.

The days were frightfully hot in Canaan. At noon Abraham would often sit in the shade of his tent, sometimes sleeping, sometimes gazing across the land. He was an old man with much of the past, and even more of the future, upon his mind.

One day Abraham noticed three strangers coming toward him. He was by habit a very good host, so he ran through the heat to greet the men and to offer them something to eat.

After finishing the meal Sarah and Abraham had prepared, one of the strangers said, "One year from now, I will pass this way again. By then Sarah will have delivered a son." Nearby, inside the tent, Sarah heard the announcement...and laughed. But the stranger silenced her laughter by asking, "Is anything too hard for the Lord?"

Suddenly Abraham knew the divine authority of his guests. Just as suddenly, one guest, the Lord himself, spoke of other things. God was distressed at the utter sinfulness of Sodom and Gomorrah, so he was going to destroy both cities with a single blow.

Abraham leaped to his feet. "My nephew!" he cried. "My

nephew Lot lives in Sodom! Will you show mercy to Lot?"

The other two had already turned to go. Their faces set to the east, they were walking toward Sodom. Abraham, wringing his hands, remained behind with the Lord.

"I will," said the Lord. Then he turned from Abraham and went his way.

Near evening the two angels of the Lord entered Sodom and went to Lot's house. The angels pleaded with Lot to leave Sodom, but he was not quickly convinced. The next morning, the angels dragged Lot and his family to the city gate. "Run to the hills," they ordered. "Run and do not look back to this place again!"

As soon as Lot and his family reached safety, God rained down sulfur and fire on Sodom and Gomorrah. Every living thing in the two cities died. In spite of the angels' warning, Lot's wife turned to look back at her city in flames. It was her last glance, a fatal glance, for she turned into a pillar of salt.

Within a year the Lord God kept his promise to Abraham. To a man one hundred years old and to his wife, ninety, God granted a miracle. To Abraham and Sarah, God gave a son.

Remembering that Sarah had laughed in the tent while the Lord sat outside, they named the boy Isaac. Isaac means "laughter."

Sarah, Abraham's wife, lived 127 years, and then she died. Abraham mourned her death but knew that the family must go on. So when the time came that his son should marry, the old man sent a servant back to the land he had left so long ago. From among Abraham's relatives the servant found a wife for Isaac. Her name was Rebekah. A dear and faithful woman, she was quick to come to Canaan.

Eventually Abraham followed Sarah. In the 175th year of his life, he breathed his last and died. An old man full of years, Abraham died and was buried alongside his wife.

A Tale of Two Brothers

Even as Abraham and Sarah had to wait a long time before Isaac was born to them, so Isaac and Rebekah had to wait for their children. Rebekah, like Sarah, was an older woman when finally she conceived. But in time, Rebekah delivered twins, each of them a boy.

The first child was ruddy and covered with red hair. He was named Esau. The second came out grabbing his brother's heel in a tight grip, as though he wanted something, as though he wanted to be first! So the second child was named Jacob, which means "grabs the heel."

Now Esau grew into a cunning hunter, ranging the fields and the forests to catch all manner of animals. But Jacob grew up a quiet man, one well contented to dwell in tents.

Isaac loved his rugged son the most because he ate what Esau hunted. But Rebekah loved Jacob.

In those days, a father willed all his wealth to his eldest son. That was the son's right by birth, his birthright. One day Jacob caught Esau at a weak moment and persuaded Esau to give him the birthright—in exchange for a pot of stew. But Jacob didn't stop at that. He and his mother conspired together to trick blind, old Isaac into giving Jacob the fatherly blessing that was also meant for the firstborn.

When Esau discovered the trickery, he wept... and hated Jacob with all his might. "When my father is dead," he vowed, "I will kill my brother. I will murder Jacob!"

How thin the walls of tents! Someone overheard Esau's threat and immediately reported it to Rebekah. Quickly she ran to Jacob, and, in words both low and urgent, she told him to escape. "To Haran," she said. "To my brother Laban's house, where you will be safe from your brother's angry hand. Go, Jacob. Go!"

So Jacob fled. One night on his long journey, he had a dream. Angels were ascending and descending a ladder whose top reached into heaven. Then God appeared to Jacob:

"I am the Lord," he proclaimed, "the God of your fathers Abraham and Isaac. I am the Lord, and I shall be your God, too. The land that you lie on I will give to your children and to your children's children; your family, who shall be as countless as the dust on earth, will be a blessing for all the families of the world. Jacob! Jacob! I am with you!"

In the morning Jacob set up the great stone that had been his pillow, poured oil over it, and bowed down to pray.

"God, I have heard you. Keep me as you promised. Take me one day back to my father's house in peace. Be with me, and you shall surely be my God."

Jacob stood up and named the place where he had slept,

where he had seen God, Bethel: "the house of God."

Soon after Jacob reached his uncle Laban, he fell in love with Laban's lovely younger daughter, Rachel. Laban agreed that Jacob could marry her if he first worked for Laban for seven years. But after the seven years were up, Laban tricked Jacob into marrying his older daughter, Leah. Laban then allowed Jacob to marry Rachel also, but only if Jacob promised seven more years of labor.

In time Jacob's family grew: eleven sons and a daughter during the time that he lived with his uncle Laban.

In all the years Jacob lived with his uncle, the love between them grew less and less. Yet Laban needed his nephew's skills. Laban's flocks and herds were thriving and expanding under Jacob's care, and Laban liked it that way.

But eventually Jacob began to raise livestock for himself, and soon he became a wealthy man with great flocks and herds of his own.

Finally the Lord God spoke the words Jacob had been waiting for: "Go home." Jacob rejoiced at the command. He waited until his uncle had gone to shear sheep; then, gathering his wives, his children, and his flocks, he fled once again.

When Jacob drew near to his brother's land, to his own homeland, there came a message to him out of that land. "Esau is coming to meet you, and he brings with him four hundred men!"

"O Lord God!" prayed Jacob. "Esau comes to kill me, my wives, and my children! I know that I am not worthy of all the mercies you have given me. I left alone; I am returning rich in family and possessions. Yet I remember your promise to me, so

I ask that you deliver me from the hand of my brother."

That night a man came to Jacob. The man wrestled with him. From midnight until morning, the two of them sweated and fought in grim silence. Like a giant, Jacob gripped his adversary; like lightning, the other slipped free and struck him back, wrenching Jacob's thigh out of joint. But Jacob locked so tight a hold on him that the other cried out, "Let me go!"

"No!" Jacob growled in his ear. "Not until you bless me."

"What is your name?" the other asked.

"I am Jacob."

"Ahh, the Grabber!" breathed the other. "Grabber, listen to me. Your name is Jacob no longer. It shall be Israel, for you have struggled with God and with humans, and you have prevailed."

With God! Jacob had struggled with God!

He dropped his hold and marveled. "I have seen God face to face," he exclaimed, "yet my life was preserved!"

With the morning, Jacob, no longer fearful of the meeting, arose and went forth gently to meet his brother.

"Jacob! Jacob!" Esau cried, as they ran together. Then Esau fell on his brother, not in anger, but in love. They embraced. They wept at the meeting. And Jacob—who was no longer Jacob, but Israel—said, "Truly, seeing your face is like seeing the face of God, my friend, my brother. No longer my enemy."

Israel. His name would stay with his family, even when they had become the multitude God had promised they would be. From this time on, they knew themselves as his children, the children of Israel.

The Family Goes to Egypt

Joseph was Israel's eleventh son but the firstborn of Rachel, Israel's most beloved wife. Therefore, to the great bitterness of his older brothers, Joseph became his father's favorite. Joseph and Benjamin—Israel's last child and Rachel's child, too—were dear and cherished in their father's eyes.

When Joseph was seventeen years old, Israel gave him a special coat, a coat ornate and beautiful. So his brothers hated him all the more and could not speak peacefully to him.

Their hatred grew dangerous when Joseph told his brothers about his dreams. In the dreams he seemed to scorn them.

"We were in a wheat field, bundling up the stalks of grain," Joseph told them. "My bundle stood up straight while yours drooped. It looked to me as though your bundles were bowing down to mine."

"So it looks to you!" they sneered at him. "It looks to you as though you will one day rule over us? Little brother, that is not how it looks to us!"

Soon Joseph was back with another dream.

"I dreamed . . ." he began.

"What, again?" they cried. "Dream, dream! Forget your dreams!"

But Joseph did not forget them. He told them instead.

"I dreamed about the sun and the moon and eleven stars. They were all bowing down . . . to me."

His brothers burned with hatred against him; even his father was hurt. "Joseph, are you suggesting," asked Israel, "that your mother and I shall bow down to you as well?"

Once when Joseph's older brothers were out watching over their father's sheep, Israel sent Joseph out to check up on them. Because of their hatred for Joseph, they saw his visit as a perfect opportunity to get rid of him. "Let's kill him!" they cried. "Let's kill him and see what becomes of his dreams!" But two of Joseph's brothers, Reuben and Judah, didn't want to see him killed. So the brothers sold Joseph to slave traders headed for Egypt. Then they took Joseph's beautiful coat, dipped it in animal blood, and sent it home to their father.

"My son!" the old man cried. "Joseph! My son! Torn to pieces by some wild beast! My son! I will never see you again!"

Regardless of what his brothers thought of him, Joseph was a gifted lad: obedient, handsome, thoughtful, wise, reliable. So the traders had no trouble selling him, and that they did to one Potiphar, a captain of Pharaoh's guard.

But such gifts are sometimes a blessing and sometimes a curse. Potiphar recognized Joseph's wisdom and put him in charge of all his household.

Unfortunately, Potiphar's wife noticed Joseph, too, and that spelled trouble. Day after day Joseph resisted her advances and refused to sin against his God. Then one day Potiphar's wife grabbed Joseph by his cloak and tried to force him to sleep with her. Joseph ran, leaving the garment in her hands.

The woman stared at the empty cloth in her hand; then she started to scream. She was humiliated! She would hurt this slave for hurting her! "Save me, save me, save me!" she shrieked.

Servants burst into the house, and she waved the empty cloak in their faces. "See this?" she cried. "Proof! The slave Joseph tried to rape me! But I screamed, and he ran away, leaving his garment behind."

Everyone believed her story. Her husband was so enraged that he had Joseph dragged away and thrown into prison.

But even in prison Joseph felt God at his side. The keeper of the prison recognized Joseph's talents and put all the prisoners into Joseph's care. Joseph came to know every man in the place, and every man came to trust him.

Some of the prisoners even told Joseph their dreams— they knew God helped him interpret dreams. Once Joseph told a former official in Pharaoh's court that his dream meant he would soon be released from prison and restored to his royal position. Within three days it all came true, just as Joseph had said. But the official, when he was set free, soon forgot about Joseph in prison.

For two long years he forgot about Joseph. But when Pharaoh was plagued by frightening dreams that none of his wise men could interpret, the official suddenly remembered Joseph. Desperate for help, Pharaoh summoned Joseph and told him his frightful dreams.

With God's help, Joseph interpreted the dreams. He explained that seven years of bounty were on the horizon but that they would be followed by seven years of famine. Therefore, Pharaoh should set someone in charge of all the harvest, someone who would gather extra in the years of plenty to be available for the years of famine.

Pharaoh nodded and whispered in wonder, "Surely, the Spirit of God is in this man." Then he put Joseph in charge of the harvest.

So Joseph, the eleventh son of Israel, went out into the land of Egypt with the power of Pharaoh and the blessing of Almighty God. He was the second in command, so people did as he ordered them to do. For seven years they stored their wonderful harvests in bins in every city of Egypt. The grain piled up beyond measure until it seemed like sand on a seashore. Joseph managed everything with a godly skill.

Then came the famine. It was everywhere. People were dying of hunger even in Joseph's homeland of Canaan. But in Egypt there was food from the earlier years of plenty. So one day Joseph's ten older brothers bowed before a governor in Egypt to ask if they could buy food. The governor—Joseph—recognized them immediately, but they did not recognize him. He sold them food, but then accused them of being spies and demanded that they return with the younger brother they had spoken of, with Benjamin.

Some time later, when the food they'd purchased was running out, the brothers prepared to return to Egypt for more. But Israel didn't want to let Benjamin go. "If he doesn't go, we won't be able to buy food," pleaded the brothers. "Then we will all surely die."

"Die?" the old man wailed. "My Joseph is gone. I couldn't bear to lose Benjamin, too. Then I would surely die!" But grudgingly the old man gave in.

When Israel's sons met the governor, no one noticed him

fighting back tears as he spoke with Benjamin. But when Joseph discovered that his brothers' hearts had truly changed—that they were sorry for what they had done to him and to their father—he could contain himself no longer.

"Leave the room!" he commanded his servants. Then, when he was alone with his brothers, he burst into loud sobbing. With tears in his eyes, he went to Judah and embraced him, to Benjamin and kissed him, and then to each of his brothers one after the other.

"I am Joseph," he said. "Look at me, Reuben—I am your brother! Judah, I am not dead, not dead at all, but alive. Levi, Dan, Simeon, it is Joseph! And you do not need to be ashamed any longer for what you did. I have been in God's hands from the beginning. Gad, go tell our father that this has been the plan of the Lord. Asher, run to him! You planned evil against me, but God planned it for good so that many people should be kept alive as they are today. Naphtali, run! Issachar, Zebulun, race! Hurry! Haste! Run! And you, Benjamin, tell our father to come down and live with me!"

And so it was that all the children and grandchildren of Israel, and even the old man himself, settled together in Egypt in the land of Goshen. They raised families. They prospered. They grew wonderfully in numbers. They became a people, a vast and countless family, and they named themselves by the name of their father—Israel.

For Israel himself, his last years were his loveliest. Twelve sons were twelve again. He looked upon them all. He blessed them. And then he died in peace.

Israel Enslaved

In the centuries after Joseph invited his family to live with him in Egypt, God kept his promise: God increased the children of Israel. Seventy persons swelled into a vast family, a multitude.

They filled the land! And finally they frightened the king of Egypt, who did not remember Joseph, who had forgotten the good he had done hundreds of years before.

"They are too many, too mighty for us," this new king concluded. So he determined to hurt them first before they could hurt him.

The king of Egypt commanded that all of the rights of the Israelites be taken away. They were no longer equal to the citizens of Egypt! They were no longer free; they were slaves!

"We will break their spirits with slavery and their backs with burdens," said Pharaoh, "so they will be too weak to threaten us by their numbers."

Yet the Lord was with Israel, and a marvelous thing happened: The more Pharaoh oppressed the people, the more they multiplied! And the more they multiplied, the more they terrified Egypt!

So Pharaoh conceived a still more dreadful plan.

First he commanded the Israelite midwives to kill every Israelite baby boy as soon as he was born. But the midwives feared God more than Pharaoh, so they ignored the command. Then Pharaoh ordered everyone to throw Israelite baby boys into the Nile River.

Israelite mothers tried desperate means to save their baby

boys. One woman wove a basket and placed her baby in it. Then she floated the basket in the reeds along the river.

When Pharaoh's daughter came to the river to bathe, she found the baby and claimed him as her own. The baby's sister, watching from nearby, ran forward and asked, "Should I find a nurse for the child?"

"Please do," this highborn, important lady replied. So the baby's sister brought his own mother to nurse and nurture him. Then the daughter of Pharaoh proclaimed, "I will name him Moses because I drew him out of the water."

Moses grew to manhood in an Egyptian house and with an Egyptian education. He walked under Egyptian eyes in Egyptian riches. But he had been born, nursed, and cuddled by an Israelite! At his mother's breast he learned that his family was Israel, that Abraham, Isaac, Jacob, and Levi were his grand-fathers, and that he himself was not, nor could ever be, Egyptian.

His heart was with the slaves, with his own people.

One day as he moved among them, grieving at the diffi-cult life that they lived, he heard a cry of pain. Among the stones an Egyptian taskmaster was whipping an Israelite. Moses caught his breath; his eyes flashed. "No!" he cried in perfect fury. Throwing himself on the Egyptian, Moses killed him. Then Moses hid the body in the sand, wondering all the time if anyone had seen the murder.

On the following day Moses went out again. This time he found two Israelites fighting each other.

"How can you do this?" he pleaded as he pulled them apart. "You are brothers, not enemies! We have enemies enough!"

But one of the men jerked away. "Moses, the most high judge of us all!" he sneered. "What will you do, kill me as you killed the Egyptian?"

Moses stared at the man and thought, "The murder is known! Pharaoh will not hesitate to execute me!"

So before nightfall Moses fled the land of Egypt altogether. He went to Midian, where he hid himself and lived for many years as a simple shepherd.

God Frees the Slaves

One day while Moses was tending sheep, he saw a sudden and marvelous sight. There, on the side of a mountain, a fire! A single bush was burning—and though the bush burned, it never burned up!

Moses began to climb the mountain, the better to see this wonder. But as soon as he stepped near it, the Lord God called out of the bush: "Moses! Moses!"

The man stopped short. "Here I am."

"Do not come nearer, but take your sandals off your feet," commanded the Lord. "The ground on which you stand is sacred!"

Moses hastened to do the Lord's will, then stood very, very still. This bush burned with no common fire; it was a fire divine!

"I have seen the oppression of my people in Egypt. I know their sufferings," said the Lord, "and I have come to deliver them. And you, Moses! I will send you to Pharaoh, to my people, to lead Israel out of slavery."

But Moses was conscious of his faults, his fears, and his failings. Even now he stood with his face covered, frightened by the nearness of his God. Slowly, he shook his head. This task was too much; it was more than he could do.

"No," he said. "If I come to Israel in Egypt with such mighty news, and the people ask who sent me, I will not know your name to say it."

"I AM WHO I AM," God said. "Tell them I AM sent you. Say, 'The Lord, the God of our fathers Abraham, Isaac, and Jacob has appeared to me. He promises to set us free from slavery and to give us a good land.'"

Finally, in spite of much resistance, God convinced Moses to go and, with the help of his eloquent brother Aaron, lead God's people out of Egypt.

So it was that Moses bowed his head before the commands of the Lord. He said farewell to those whom he had come to love in Midian and returned to Egypt, to the task too great for him.

First Moses met Aaron, then together they revealed to Israel all that the Lord had spoken upon his mountain.

The children of Israel rejoiced. They were glad to learn that God cared for them, that he planned to set them free. They bowed their heads and worshiped. Then they watched as Moses and Aaron went to speak with Pharaoh...

"The Lord, the Lord God," Aaron declared before Pharaoh, "the God of Israel says, 'Let my people go that they may hold a feast for me in the wilderness!'"

Pharaoh looked on the two men standing in front of him and chuckled. "Which god did you say this was?" he asked. "I don't believe I've heard of this god before."

· "He is the God of Israel," said Aaron, "and he shall strike Egypt with disease and with the sword if his word is not obeyed."

"Do you mean," said Pharaoh, "that I should submit to a little deity—and at the same time give my slaves a rest? Get out of here! You and your little god, get out of my sight!"

But the word had been spoken: "Let my people go." And though Pharaoh did not acknowledge it, the war had begun!

As soon as Moses and Aaron left him, Pharaoh summoned the taskmasters of Israel. He ordered them to require of the Israelites the same number of bricks as always but to make the Israelites scrounge for their own straw.

When the Israelites saw Moses and Aaron again, they were furious. "You've made trouble for us with Pharaoh," they cried. "This isn't setting us free! This is putting the sword into Pharaoh's hands that he might kill us!"

They would listen no more to Moses; even Moses wondered how God would deliver the people. He wondered why God had sent him at all. For here, at the beginning, it looked as though Pharaoh were winning!

Then began the signs, the wonders, the terrors, the mighty acts of God as he fought on behalf of his people.

The Lord God turned all the water in the Nile River into blood. The canals, the ponds, the pools, the water in jugs, and the water in cups—all of it went to blood.

But when Pharaoh found that his magicians could do the same thing by their magic, he ignored Moses. Pharaoh hardened his heart and refused to let the children of Israel go anywhere.

Then God sent frogs into the land of Egypt. The earth bounced with them. The waters swarmed with them. The houses, the bedrooms, the pots, and the ovens were full of them.

This time, though Pharaoh's magicians could imitate God's miracle, they could not undo it. They could not rid the country of frogs.

So Pharaoh called for Moses and Aaron. "Is your God great enough to stop what he has started?" he demanded. "Tell him to take the frogs away, and I will let the people go."

Calmly Moses replied, "That you may know that there is no one like the Lord our God, it shall be done tomorrow."

And so it was. On the morrow the frogs died wherever they were. People shoveled them into piles as high as houses, but they could not escape the awful stench. Then Pharaoh hardened his heart again, and he would not let the people go.

So God turned the dust into gnats, and the gnats covered everything. Still Pharaoh's heart remained hard.

Next came flies—crawling, buzzing flies everywhere! Then diseases fell on the Egyptians' flocks and herds, then boils on the bodies of the Egyptians themselves. But with each of these plagues, Pharaoh's heart only got harder. He would not let God's people go.

Next came lightning and hail that battered everything—humans, animals, and crops. Only in Goshen, where the children of Israel lived, was there no hail. Still Pharaoh stubbornly refused.

So God sent clouds of locusts that ate every green thing in their path and then darkness so thick that it could be felt.

One last time Moses stood before Pharaoh.

"No! No! No! No!" Pharaoh was on his feet and shaking. "I will never let my slaves go," he cried. "Get out of my sight! Never see my face again! See me again, troubler, and you die!"

Moses said, "Just as you say, Pharaoh. I will never see your face again."

Plague after plague the children of Israel had watched in wonder. Nine signs, nine wonders, the mighty hand and the outstretched arm of the Lord their God had turned their hearts, and they no longer doubted the words of Moses. They trusted Moses, the servant of God.

Therefore, when Moses called the elders of Israel to himself, they came. When he cried silence and demanded their attention, they gave it. When he urged them to prepare for the final, most terrible plague of all, they did.

"At midnight," Moses cried, "the Lord God shall confound Pharaoh, Egypt, and the whole of the land! Not a house stands but that there shall be weeping in its walls—except, that is, for the houses of Israel! The houses of those who prepare themselves shall go untouched! God shall pass over the prepared. Therefore, Israel, prepare the Passover!"

And Israel did prepare just as Moses instructed.

At midnight, death descended on the land. At midnight, God did go throughout Egypt, killing the firstborn of every family. Of Pharaoh, the firstborn son was slain! Of the captive who sat in the dungeon, the firstborn son! Of the maid who worked at the mill, the firstborn! Of all the fathers and all the mothers throughout all of Egypt, the eldest son died. There was not a house where one was not dead.

A cry then rose up in Egypt. Wailing, weeping all the night long, tears and swollen sorrow.

Finally Pharaoh cried to Moses and Aaron, "Away! Away! You and the people of Israel, your flocks and your herds, go away and serve the Lord God as you have said!" Then softly he added, "And bless me also."

The children of Israel clapped their hands at the freedom that lay before them! Not one of their sons had died. The children of Israel grabbed the bread dough before it had time to rise, and yet while the night was upon them they left their houses. They left the cities and the land of Goshen. After four hundred years, they got up and went out of Egypt. Free, free, free at last—the children of Israel marched into the wilderness a free people!

Israel was indeed free. The wide wilderness stretched all around, and to the Lord alone were the people indebted. God was their God; him alone should they serve!

The Red Sea Miracle

In the days following their escape, the Lord led them! He went before them by day in a pillar of cloud. By night he led them with a pillar of fire that lit their way. Always he was near; always he was in front of them.

But Pharaoh of the narrow eyes, Pharaoh of the deep suspicions, Pharaoh of the fierce, unstable, hateful heart had changed his mind again.

"We must have been mad," he raged, "to let Israel go! Why did we do such a thing? Arise! After them!"

With six hundred of his finest chariots, with horses and warriors, with spears, swords, and bristling arrows, Pharaoh entered the field. Eastward he rode, his army massed and flashing behind him.

When the Israelites saw the Egyptian army behind them and a vast sea in front of them, they were terrified. All the people began to lift their voices and to cry, "Moses! Moses! Aren't there graves in Egypt? Did we have to come here to die? O God, we are all going to die!"

"Do not be afraid!" Moses cried in a ringing voice.

"But there is nothing we can do!" they shrieked.

"Then do nothing," cried Moses, "but trust! The Lord will fight for you! You have only to be still!"

The pillar of cloud rose up. It moved from the sea to a space between Israel and Egypt. It settled, hiding the people from the army, and there it stayed until the night was come.

Then, during that night of blind, furious confusion, God performed another wonder.

At the command of the Lord God Almighty, Moses stretched his hand over the sea. A strong east wind began to blow, screaming past the ears of Israel and slapping the whole water of the sea. Hard did that wind blow the long night through. It drove the waters to the left, and they piled up; it swept the waters to the right, and they piled up. It scoured the seabed dry. And while yet the wind was blowing, all the children of Israel crossed the Red Sea. They walked between the two walls of water. They walked to freedom!

As soon as the morning light appeared, Egypt saw where Israel had gone. "After them! After them!" Pharaoh roared above the streaming wind. "Arrow, strike! Sword, destroy them! After them!"

Pharaoh gave rein to his chariot horses. Their eyes rolled, their necks strained forward, and they charged forward between the walls of water. Six hundred chariots followed, horses and warriors with the weapons of death in their hands.

"After them!" Pharaoh howled, as the wheels of his heavy chariot suddenly stopped turning freely. Foot soldiers rushed past. "After them!"

Moses stood on the other side, watching the advancing army.

"Now!" the Lord God whispered. "Now, Moses, stretch your hand above the sea."

Moses stretched forth his hand above the sea, above Pharaoh, above the whole host of Egypt... and the east wind died.

In the terrible silence that followed, the walls of water, both left and right, came crashing down. The sea slammed back to its regular place, and the sea did cover Pharaoh in white water and a swirl. The sea swallowed his chariots, his horses, his armies, his officers to the last man, until not a soul was left alive. Now there was water only, the still, calm water, and Israel standing on the farther shore.

Thus the Lord saved Israel that day from the hand of the Egyptians, and Israel saw Egypt dead upon the seashore. Israel saw the great work that the Lord had done, and the people believed in the Lord and in his servant Moses.

The people believed in the Lord and in his servant Moses—for a little while.

Covenant at Sinai

Leaving the Red Sea behind, the people of Israel headed across the desert wilderness, following the cloud and the pillar of fire. Three days and three nights they walked. Then the water ran out. Children cried for a drink. Their parents complained to Moses. But God was watching. He provided sweet water for them at a bitter spring in the desert.

For another month and a half, the people traveled. But eventually they ran out of food. Soon the children were whining. Soon the people turned on Moses: "You brought us out here to kill us! If only we had died by God's hand in Egypt! There we had plenty to eat! Here we are starving!"

But God again would be faithful. "In the morning," Moses answered, "you shall see the glory of the Lord. You shall know that he is the Lord your God!"

In the morning, in the sweet beginning of the day, the wide face of the wilderness was lacy white. "What is it?" they asked. It tasted like wafers made with honey. This food that God had provided for them they called manna, their term for "What is it?" It appeared every morning without fail all the years they wandered in the wilderness.

That should have been the end of their complaining, but it wasn't. Again the water ran out, and again the people confronted Moses—this time with stones in their hands and murder in their eyes. But again God provided water. That should have ended the complaining—but it didn't.

On and on the children of Israel traveled through the wilderness until one month had become two, and two, three. Finally they saw in the distance a singular mountain. In sight of this stony majesty they paused...

God had led them here. This was a sacred mountain, God's mountain, Sinai. Here the Lord God made a covenant with his people, even as he had with their father Abraham. And under this covenant he gave them his law. Israel, special unto the Lord God, was asked by God to behave in a special way.

God called Moses to come up the mountain. Moses ascended the mountain alone and was swallowed in cloud.

Then God spoke all these words, saying,

"I am the Lord your God, who brought you out of the land of Egypt, out of the house of slavery. You shall have no other gods before me.

"Do not make for yourself an idol or worship the likeness of anything that is created. You shall not bow down to any image or serve it.

"Do not misuse the name of the Lord your God.

"Remember the Sabbath day as a special day. You may work six days, but the seventh day is a Sabbath to the Lord your God. On that day you shall rest, even as the Lord rested after the six days of creating, even as he rested and made that day sacred.

"Honor your father and your mother, that your days may be long in the land that the Lord your God will give you.

"Do not murder.

"Do not commit adultery.

"Do not steal.

"Do not testify falsely against your neighbor.

"Do not crave your neighbor's house nor desire his wife, his servants, or his property. Do not long for anything that belongs to your neighbor."

These ten commands the Lord God spoke in Moses' hearing that the people might obey and live as God's own people.

Then the Lord gave Moses many other ordinances, laws, and rules so that the people might live peacefully with one another.

When Moses returned and told the people all the words of the Lord, they all answered with one voice, "All the words that the Lord has spoken, we will do!"

Then Moses left the people behind, again to enter the cloud alone. This time he was gone long, long from the people—forty days and forty nights upon the mountain.

Again God spoke. Steadily, carefully, in painstaking detail, God described for Moses the tabernacle where Israel was to worship, the shrine where God would meet his people. He gave Moses instructions for every part of it, including the furniture it would contain and the ark of the covenant, an ornate chest to hold the stone tablets on which God would inscribe his law. God listed for Moses the holy festivals that Israel was to keep every year.

When he had made an end of speaking on the mountain, God finally gave to Moses the two tablets of stone, the tablets on which the Lord God himself had written his law.

The Golden Calf

"Where's Moses?"

"Gone! Maybe he's lost; maybe he's dead—who knows?"

"Oh, where *is* Moses?"

"Gone! Gone!"

Thus spoke all the people of Israel among themselves. Worried, lonely, frightened, and full of woe, they suffered in the absence of the man who made decisions for them.

"Where is Moses? Where is God?"

"Aaron!" they said, when finally they had made up their minds. "We can't go on like this. We need a god who will go before us and lead us. Aaron, make us a god!"

Aaron, the brother of Moses, agreed. At his command, all the people of Israel took the gold rings from their ears and brought them to him.

Aaron melted all this gold. He formed it, fashioned it, carved it, and made from it an idol in the shape of a calf.

When he brought the calf before the people, they clapped their hands and cried, "Here is our god, the one who led us out of Egypt!" Then they worshiped the thing they had made.

As Moses descended the mountain, he heard a curious noise. It was a wine-driven cry from the camp below. Suddenly Moses spied the golden calf, and anger erupted in his soul.

Moses raised the two tablets of stone above his head. Down they came with a mighty crack! He broke them at the foot of the mountain—and the people knew that Moses had returned.

Seizing the calf, Moses burned it with fire, then ground it

to powder and scattered it upon the water. "Drink!" Moses commanded, and the people of Israel drank.

"Now, who is on the Lord's side?" cried Moses, standing at the entrance to the camp. "Come to me!"

All the men of the tribe of Levi stepped away from the people and gathered around Moses.

"This is what the Lord God of Israel says," Moses told the Levites. "Take your swords. Go back and forth from gate to gate throughout the whole camp, and each of you kill your brother, your companion, and your neighbor!"

As God commanded, so did the sons of Levi. There fell dead three thousand men that day because the sin Israel had committed had been serious. Israel had rejected God's law. With their golden calf, they had rejected God himself!

Moses hated the golden calf, but he hurt for his people and grieved for the harm they had done to themselves. So the prophet of God trudged back up the mountain of God and sought to speak with the Lord once again, this time to pray for Israel.

God loved his people and trusted his prophet, so he accepted Moses' prayer. The Lord changed his mind concerning the evil that he thought to do to his people. Instead, he forgave Israel.

"I am the Lord, the great I AM!" proclaimed God. "I am a God merciful and gracious, slow to anger and abounding in constant love and faithfulness, forgiving iniquity and transgressions and sin. But I am a God who will by no means let sin go unpunished!"

Then, to show that he had truly forgiven Israel, God told Moses to write the Ten Commandments—God's law—on two more tablets of stone, just like the first. With these tablets in hand, Moses returned to the people and said:

"Now, Israel, what does the Lord your God require of you, but to reverence him, to walk in all his ways, to love him, to serve him with all your heart, and to keep his commands? Love, therefore, the Lord your God! And be no longer stubborn. For the Lord is God of gods and Lord of lords, the great, the mighty, the awe-inspiring God. He is your God, who has done for you these great and wonderful things!"

Once again the nation began moving. They were moving toward the land that God had promised to Abraham centuries before—Canaan. The promised land! Israel's family was going home.

The Lost Generation

Now the Lord God had promised that manna would cover the ground as long as the people journeyed through the wilderness. Faithful the word of their merciful God! The morning earth was always white with the sweet, melting food. The people always ate. The people never went hungry.

But some of the people grew bored.

"Leeks!" somebody grumbled. "Leeks, onions, garlic—something else!" And someone, with a faraway look in his eyes, cried, "Melons! Cucumbers!" Somebody else added, "Fish!" Then they all began to moan, "Meat! We want meat!

We want to chew and taste the stuff we eat. Meat!"

The Lord grew tired of Israel's constant complaining. "They want meat?" God said to Moses. "Then they shall have meat!"

An east wind began to blow and with it came birds. Exhausted and helpless in the strong wind, thousands upon thousands of quail were blown straight at Israel. Then the quail dropped from the sky until they piled up to people's waists! Meat for the picking. Meat so abundant that some people ate until they were sick. Some even died as punishment from God. They named that place "Graves of Craving" to remind the people of their sin.

When Israel encamped south of Canaan, excitement spread through the camp. Moses was sending spies into the promised land, one from each of the twelve tribes! Forty days later when the spies returned, the excitement grew, for they brought with them the fruits of a plentiful land. Unfortunately, they also brought a dreadful report: The land was filled with walled cities and gigantic warriors. "It's no good! No good!" they cried. "We can't conquer giants!"

Of the twelve spies, only Caleb and Joshua remained confident that the Lord could conquer the giants for them. But the people listened to the other ten, complaining once more that God had freed them from slavery in Egypt.

God was furious. "How long will this people despise me?" the Lord God thundered. "Stand aside—I'll destroy them all!" Moses held his ground. Then softly, quietly, Moses reasoned with the Lord and convinced him not to destroy his own people.

Then the Lord said to Moses, "As I live, not one of the people who have seen my marvelous works and who yet have not believed in me—not one of them shall see the land that I promised to their ancestors! As I live," vowed the Lord, "their dead bodies shall fall in this wilderness. Those who murmured against me shall wander forty years until the last of their number is gone. Their children, Caleb, and Joshua shall enter the land of promise, but not the ones who murmured."

Sadly Moses turned and told the people all the words that the Lord had spoken.

Forty years, a full generation, the children of Israel wandered the wilderness. Many died along the way. Many were born. Often they repeated their rebellious ways, but every time they did, the Lord drew them back to himself with discipline and love.

He tested them to discover what was in their hearts, whether they would keep his commands or not. He taught them that no one lives by bread alone but by everything that proceeds out of the mouth of the Lord.

Their clothing did not wear out. Their feet did not swell those forty years. Slowly, slowly the children of Israel learned to turn to the Lord their God, to trust in him, and to live.

And so it was that the children of Israel were changed!

For the more they trusted the Lord their God to lead them, the mightier was their sword, the more frightful their armies!

They went into the wilderness a trembling people. They came out of it a fit and fateful nation!

So Israel stood ready to enter Canaan, the land of promise.

But Moses, 120 years old, was not to go along. His time and his duties were done—well done. So Joshua, the son of Nun, was appointed by the Lord God to lead Israel into the land.

Yet one more time before his old eyes closed, one last time before he died, Moses spoke to all the people.

"Hear, O Israel! Love the Lord your God. Serve him with all your heart and soul. Then God will give the rain for your land in its season, that you may gather in your grain and enjoy your wine and your oil. Walk in the ways of the Lord your God; cling to him alone. Do not turn aside to worship other gods! Then every place on which you step will be your own. No one will be able to stand against you! The Lord will lay the fear of you upon all the land where you walk."

Then Moses raised his hands and blessed them.

"Blessed are you, O Israel!" he said. "Who is like you, a people saved by the Lord? May the eternal God be your dwelling place, his everlasting arms your sure foundation."

Finally Moses left them on the plain, and for the last time he climbed a mountain alone. Up Mount Nebo he went to the very peak. Then after viewing the land of promise in the distance, Moses died and was buried in a place known only to God. There has never arisen since then a prophet in Israel like Moses, with whom the Lord spoke face to face.

Israel Conquers Canaan

"Moses, my servant, is dead," the Lord God reminded Joshua, the son of Nun. Joshua bowed his head. The voice of

Almighty God is an awesome thing.

"Be strong, Joshua! Be of good courage!" said the Lord. "For you shall lead this people into the land that I swore I would give to their ancestors. Be strong, taking care to obey all that Moses commanded you. Be brave, for no adversary shall be able to stand before you all the days of your life. As I was with Moses, so shall I be with you. I will never forsake you!"

So Joshua called two men to himself. "Carefully, quietly," he said, "like whispering shadows pass through the land, slip into the city Jericho. Determine its strength and discover its weakness, then bring your report to me."

The men melted into darkness and stole into Jericho, the first major city across the Jordan River. There they found the walls to be a thick, unassailable protection all around the city.

There the two spies also took refuge in the house of Rahab, a prostitute. The king of Jericho was looking for the spies, but Rahab feared God more than the king, so she hid them under stalks of flax that were laid out to dry on her roof.

Later, before the spies made their escape, they promised to reward Rahab for her bravery. If Rahab would tie a red cord in her window, she and her entire family would be spared the coming destruction. Rahab and her loved ones would escape when Israel put the rest of the city to the sword and to the flames.

Three days the spies hid in the hills. But when they returned to Joshua, they brought a joyful report: The citizens of Jericho were afraid of the Israelites, for they had heard how God fought for Israel! The walls of Jericho were strong and thick, but the people inside were faint of heart.

So Joshua led the people to the eastern shore of the Jordan River. Here they stared at the river in silence.

It was spring. The northern snows were melting, and the river that cut between them and the land of promise was flooding! Its waters ran high and hard, growling at the banks and swelling in the middle. There was no bridge. There was no shallow place to ford the raging river.

But God was with Joshua as he had been with Moses. At Joshua's instruction, the priests carrying the ark of the covenant stepped into the edge of the rushing waters. Suddenly the river shrank before them. It became a stream. Then a creek, then a gentle brook. By the time the priests reached the center, the river had stopped altogether! So the priests carrying the ark stood in the center of the riverbed while all the people of Israel crossed over it.

As soon as the priests' feet left the riverbed, the water flowed again. The Jordan again became a furious, flooding, rushing river. Awed by the sight, the people piled up stones they had taken from the riverbed to remind them of all God had done for them.

Safely across the Jordan, Israel was ready to advance to Jericho. Yet it was not Joshua, their commander, but the Lord their God who planned by peculiar stratagem to crush the city Jericho. The battle was one of awesome power and almighty mystery.

Early one morning the watchmen of Jericho leaned over the walls to see a strange sight. Israel's warriors were marching... but not to the attack!

In perfect order, in dreadful silence, and staring straight ahead, the warriors marched around the city. In their midst was the ark of the covenant; before the ark marched seven priests dressed in white. Then all at once the seven priests raised curved rams' horns to their lips.

The trumpets blew a chilling sound. Jericho gasped. But the warriors of Israel did not break stride. Marching, marching under the trumpet blasts of the glory of God, surrounding the ark of his presence, marching, until once they had circled the city, then silently marching away, back to their camp—that was all Israel did.

The day was still again. The plains outside the city were empty: footprints, but no feet; memory of the mysterious procession, but no warriors, no priests, no ark.

What was Israel doing?

The next morning the warriors and the priests of Israel appeared again, marched the same course around the city, again blasting the rams' horns but uttering no human sound, no shout, no word, no whisper.

What was Israel doing?

And on the third day, and on the fourth, and the fifth, and the sixth, the same mysterious march. Israel—what?

But for the seventh day the Lord had given other instructions to his warriors, and on the seventh day his terrible might burst forth upon the city Jericho.

At sunrise Israel emerged from camp and marched as they had before, but this time once around was not enough. They circled the city a second time, a third, a fourth...

Then, on the seventh time around, Joshua threw back his head and called, "Shout, warriors! Shout your battle cry! For the Lord has given you the city!"

The warriors raised a great shout. They roared. Their voices shook the air with a terrible cry—and the walls of the city fell down flat. Then every warrior turned his face toward Jericho. Every warrior leaped the crumbled stone of the walls, entered, and fought—and utterly destroyed all in the city.

Only Rahab and her family were brought out alive before Joshua burned the city and cursed it for all time.

A mighty wonder of God: The door to Canaan, the way into the land of promise, was open to Israel. So the Lord God was with Joshua, and his fame spread throughout all the land.

A long time Joshua made war against all the kings of Canaan. But eventually he took the whole land, according to all that the Lord had spoken. When he was done, the land was divided among the tribes of Israel, and the land had rest from war.

"Thus says the Lord, the God of Israel, 'I gave you a land on which you have not labored, and in cities that you did not build, you dwell. You eat the fruit of vineyards and olive groves that you did not plant!' "

So began Joshua's last words to the children of Israel. When he was an old man and when all the people of Israel had settled snugly into their new home, he called them to Shechem, where he spoke these final words to them.

"Therefore, fear the Lord," he commanded, "and serve him in sincerity. Put away false gods. However, if you are unwilling to serve the Lord, choose this day whom you will serve, whether the false gods of your ancestors or the idols once served in this land. But as for me and my house, we will serve the Lord."

The people answered, "Far be it from us to forsake the Lord to serve other gods. We also will serve the Lord, for he is our God!"

After these things, Joshua died—Joshua, the son of Nun and the servant of the Lord, a man full of strength and courage, 110 years old.

God Angry, God Merciful

By the might of the Lord, Israel had conquered Canaan and made it their own. But matters did not stay calm and so clear, for Israel had not cleared the land of all the Canaanites! In pockets throughout the land, in cities and on the high places, the enemy continued to dwell side by side with Israel and continued to worship their own gods, the Baals.

"The more I call my people Israel," said the Lord with sorrow, "the more they go from me. They keep sacrificing to the Baals and burning incense to idols."

That was the evil Moses had commanded them not to do; that was the gross wickedness Joshua had warned against. Yet the people did it anyway. They forsook their God. So God, in his anger, withdrew his protective arms from around them.

When the Lord no longer shielded Israel, enemies unkind and murderous swept down on his people, marauding the land and killing them. So Israel bled. Israel groaned. Israel cried out to the Lord God for mercy.

Hearing the cry of his people, God would send his Spirit to raise up among the people a judge, someone to gather them together into a hard army. Then the army of Israel would, by the strength of the Lord, defeat this enemy. The land would enjoy peace again . . . for a little while.

Only a little while. For this is the poor story that was repeated again and again with one generation after another: that Israel would anger God by forsaking him; that God would permit some enemy to grieve Israel; that Israel, oppressed, would plead to God for mercy; that God would save the people of Israel through the leadership of a judge— and then that Israel would anger God by forsaking him . . .

During this period of Israel's history, God raised up many judges to rescue the people of Israel from their oppressors. Deborah directed an army of ten thousand to defeat a Canaanite army. Gideon—with three hundred men and a miracle of God—drove the Midianites and the Amalekites from the land. And Samson, through his God-given strength, killed thousands of the Philistines who were constantly raiding Israel. Through these and many other judges, God showed his faithfulness to Israel and sought to draw the people closer to himself.

Israel Asks for a King

Samuel, God's prophet, was Israel's last and greatest judge. Many times God had helped Israel defeat the Philistines, but these tyrants just would not go away. Eventually the people grew restless. All around them the nations had kings to rule them, to lead them into battle. Israel had no king but God. Perhaps a king would deliver them from Philistine oppression. "Appoint a king for us," the people demanded of Samuel.

Displeased, Samuel reminded them of the taxes and the hardships a king would inevitably impose on them. But the people would not relent. So Samuel took their request to God.

"They have not rejected you," God informed Samuel. "They have rejected me from being king over them. Do what they say. Give them their king."

Saul was a handsome man. When he walked among the people, his head and shoulders rose higher than the head of any other. There was a strong and urgent fire in his face—he could charm, he could excite, he could inspire. He looked like a king.

Yet for all his marvelous talent, Saul was a marvelous failure.

His reign began well, for under Saul Israel defeated many enemies. Saul created a standing army, and with that army he and his son Jonathan defended Israel. However, Saul placed more confidence in his military might than he did in God.

To make matters worse, Saul feared the people more than he feared the Lord. Once Saul and his army assembled for battle against the Philistines. But Samuel was late. He had not yet arrived to offer the pre-battle sacrifice.

With every passing minute, Saul grew more nervous. His troops began to desert him—so Saul himself seized wood and meat, and Saul himself made the offering to the Lord. Immediately Samuel appeared in the camp, furious. "What

1 SAMUEL 8–9; 13

have you done?" he demanded. "You have not kept the command of the Lord. You took rights unto yourself that were not yours for the taking! You have sinned!"

The Lord delivered Israel that day, but he was displeased because Saul offered the sacrifice on his own, because Saul disobeyed his clear command. It was the first of many such days to come in the reign of Saul.

Not once, but again and again Saul listened to the people first and to the Lord second.

Finally the word of the Lord came to Samuel. "I regret ever making Saul king! He has turned away from me and has not performed my commandments!"

It became Samuel's sad duty, then, to convey this hard word to Saul. "Hear what the Lord said to me just this night," he began.

Saul lowered his head and whispered, "Say on."

"Obedience is better than sacrifice," Samuel continued, "and following God is better than offering him gifts. Because you have rejected the word of the Lord, he has also rejected you as king."

The urgent fire that once burned so boldly in Saul's face did not go out. But it changed. It grew dark. It turned inward, and sometimes it caused him a most desperate pain. From that time on, one thing alone did ease the poor king's soul: music.

Therefore, Saul's attendants brought him David, the son of Jesse, to play soothing music for Saul on the lyre. Saul didn't know that this same David had already been anointed by Samuel to replace Saul. Young David was to be the next king of Israel.

David the Giant-Killer

Now the Philistines mustered again for war. (Saul was never, in all his days, able to crush this enemy once and for all.) They drew up their armies on one mountain, while Saul gathered the Israelite forces on another. The Valley of Elah lay between them.

"Hear, O Israel!" boomed a voice from the valley every day. "Hear, you insects of Saul! Listen, you grasshoppers!" The Israelite warriors heard the taunts every day, and every day for forty days they clung to the side of the mountain and cowered in fear.

Because it was the voice of a giant. "I am Goliath of Gath!" he roared. Nearly ten feet tall, a helmet of bronze on his head, a coat of mail covering his torso, bronze plates protecting his legs, a bronze javelin slung down between his shoulders, a spear whose shaft was like a weaver's beam and whose iron head weighed fifteen pounds—this was Goliath of Gath!

"I defy the armies of Israel!" he thundered. "Give me a man that we may fight! Israel, send me your champion!"

But there was no champion in Israel willing to look at the Philistine giant up close.

There was only the boy David, who finally approached King Saul in his tent.

Saul agreed to let David go and fight the giant. He dressed the boy in his own armor and strapped his sword to David's side. "Go, and the Lord be with you," he encouraged. But David could barely move. All that metal was more than the boy could bear. So David took it off, picked up only his staff, his shepherd's pouch, his sling, and, from a nearby brook, five smooth stones. Lightly he descended to the valley below.

Goliath was waiting in his usual spot. Then suddenly he saw a boy walking his way.

He might have laughed at the little figure, as if this were a joke. Instead, the giant glared, insulted. "Am I a dog," he growled, "that you come at me with sticks?" He began to curse David by all his gods, but the boy walked on with his sling, his stones, and no fear in his face.

Then David spoke. "You come against me with a sword and a spear and a javelin," he said, "but I come to you in the name of the Lord of the armies of Israel. This day the Lord will deliver you into my hand, that all the earth may know there is a God in Israel! The battle is the Lord's. The battle is the Lord's."

David ran quickly, lightly, to meet the Philistine. He put his hand in his bag, took out a stone. The sling made a small buzz as David whirled it around his head, a snap when he let it go. The stone struck Goliath on the forehead and sank into his skull. The giant fell like lumber to the ground.

Immediately David ran and stood over the Philistine. David had no sword . . . but Goliath did. Drawing Goliath's sword out of its sheath, David killed the Philistine hero, then cut off his head with his own sword.

When the Philistines saw their champion dead, they broke ranks and ran. The men of Israel pursued them as far as Gath and killed them up to the gates of Ekron. David brought the head of the giant back to camp, but he kept the Philistine's weapons for himself.

It was then that King Saul began to love David less, for all of the people praised their hero—the one who had killed the Philistine hero—but few of the people praised their king.

One morning, when darkness smothered his spirit and rage smoldered in his heart, when David was playing the lyre to soothe him, Saul screamed, grabbed a spear, and threw it at David. "I'll pin him to the wall!" he thought. But David evaded him twice and sadly fled the presence of his king.

Hotter and hotter burned the fire in Saul's face. The man was nearly mad with yearning to see David dead. So every time someone reported, "David is here!" or "David is there!" Saul led his troops in furious pursuit of his enemy, to hunt David, to kill David.

It was in the southern part of the kingdom that Saul had pursued David, but one day the king and his armies marched to the north, as far as Jezreel. There the Philistines had gathered their forces for war, to fight against Israel.

Across the valley, Saul looked and saw the Philistine battle lines, their hundreds and their thousands. He trembled at the sight. The king was afraid.

Again and again Saul asked the Lord for some word about the battle to come. But Saul received no answer. Neither by dreams nor by the prophets would God break his silence. The Lord had left him. Saul was utterly alone.

Desperate, Saul secretly consulted a witch, even though it was against God's command and Saul's own law to do so. Saul wanted to speak with Samuel, who had died some years ago.

Out of the dark, up from the ground, Samuel appeared to

deliver a message to Saul—the following day the battle would be lost, and Saul and his sons would die.

The next day it was just as Samuel had said. The Philistines fought against Israel, and the men of Israel either fled or fell dead on the face of Mount Gilboa. Dead were the sons of Saul. Dead! And dead lay Jonathan among them.

Saul, grievously wounded by arrows and aware that there was no escape, drew his own sword and fell upon it.

When David heard of the terrible defeat and of the death of the king, he took hold of his clothes and tore them. David mourned for Saul, and for Jonathan he wept.

God Gives Israel His King

David, the son of Jesse, born in Bethlehem, of the tribe of Judah—David had a strong right arm, a shrewd mind, and a generous heart.

David also sought to please God. Throughout his life David expressed his feelings to God in song, songs to tell God his joys, his sorrows, his concerns. Once David wrote:

"The Lord is my shepherd; I shall not want. He makes me lie down in green pastures; he leads me beside still waters. He restores my soul. He leads me in right paths for his name's sake. Even though I walk through the darkest valley, I fear no evil; for you are with me; your rod and your staff, they comfort me. You prepare a table before me in the presence of my enemies; you anoint my head with oil; my cup overflows! Surely goodness and mercy will follow me all the days of my life, and I will dwell in the house of the Lord forever."

With all of his heart, and with all of his soul, and with all of his might, King David loved the Lord.

After defeating the Philistines once and for all, David steadily expanded his little kingdom by subduing all the peoples surrounding Israel. They all became his servants, for the Lord gave victory to David wherever he went. The Lord made Israel, under David, an empire that ruled lands north and east and south for as far as the eye could see.

Thus did the Lord God keep the promise he had made a thousand years before: "Arise, Abraham. Walk through the land, for I will give it to you and to your descendants!"

So David reigned. So David administered justice and equity to all his people.

Now Hiram, king of Tyre, had given David a present: a palace built of cedar trees and stone. In the cool of the evening, David would often stroll on the roof of his house and gaze down upon his city, upon Jerusalem.

One evening David looked down from his rooftop and spied a beautiful woman bathing in her courtyard pool. Her name was Bathsheba, and her husband, Uriah, was away fighting the Ammonites for David and for Israel. "Bring her to me," David ordered a servant. Bathsheba came, and David slept with her. Then she returned to her own home. Some time later, she sent David a message: "I'm going to have a baby."

Seeking to hide his sin, David had Uriah brought home

from the war. But Uriah, feeling it would be unfair to his comrades in the field, refused to sleep with his wife. Now desperate, David ordered Uriah to the front lines and instructed his general to leave Uriah unprotected. Just as David planned, Uriah was killed by the enemy.

After Bathsheba had mourned for her husband, David brought her to the palace to be his wife. He had hidden his sin from his people... but not from his God.

Shortly after the child was born, Nathan the prophet came to David with a matter requiring the king's judgment. "It involves two men," Nathan explained.

"Tell me," said the king.

"One man is rich. He has many flocks and herds, and he lives in a high cedar house. The other man is poor, owning but one ewe lamb, which once he loved and raised in his house as though it were a daughter. Food from his table, drink from his cup, and a place by his side at night were all hers.

"Now this," said the prophet, "is the matter. A traveler came to the rich man, but the rich man was unwilling to kill any of his own sheep to feed his guest. Instead, he took the poor man's lamb, killed her, and fed his guest upon her sweet flesh..."

David stood up, angry with the rich man. "As the Lord lives," he said, "that man deserves to die. My judgment? That he restore the lamb fourfold because he had no pity!"

"You are the man!" Nathan declared. David sat down again. "You have many wives," said the prophet. "Uriah the Hittite had but one. Yet you killed him with the sword of the Ammonites to add his one wife to your many! You have utterly despised the Lord; therefore, the sword will never depart from your family."

When David saw his sin through God's eyes, he wept and prayed:

"Have mercy on me, O God, according to your unfailing love. According to your great compassion, erase my transgressions. For I confess my crime, and my sin is ever before me. Against you have I sinned and done this evil in your sight!

"Create in me a pure heart, O God, and renew a right spirit within me! Restore unto me the joy of your salvation, and sustain in me a willing spirit."

Then Nathan declared, "David, your sin has its consequence. But in his mercy the Lord has not turned away from you. Instead, God has put your sin away. You are forgiven. However, the son born to you and Bathsheba will die."

In time, Bathsheba bore the king a second son. They named him Solomon. This one the Lord loved dearly. David was indeed forgiven.

After many years of trusting God and ruling wisely, King David grew old and his shoulders bent down under the glory and the grief of his reign. He called Solomon to his side.

"My son, I am about to die," he said. "By my promise to you and your mother, by the anointing of Zadok the priest and the word of Nathan the prophet, by the choosing of the Lord, you shall rule this land after me.

"Solomon, be strong. Keep the laws of the Lord your God, walking in his ways and obeying his commands as they are written in the Torah, the teachings of Moses. Then you shall prosper and the promise of the Lord will most certainly be established, that a son of David will ever sit upon this throne."

Then David died and was buried in the city that bore his name, the city of David. Solomon took his place on David's throne, and Solomon's kingdom was firmly established.

David's Kingdom Crumbles

One night the Lord appeared to Solomon in a dream. "Ask for anything you want," God said. "I'll give it to you."

"Ah, my Lord," Solomon replied, "you have shown unfailing love to my father, for you have set his son upon the throne. But I am like a little child. I do not know how to be a king. Yet you have placed me in the midst of your people, a great people that cannot be numbered.

"Now show me your unfailing love. Give me an understanding mind to govern your people, the wisdom to tell right from wrong."

It pleased the Lord that Solomon had asked this. "Not long life," said the Lord. "Not riches for yourself, nor for the lives of your enemies have you asked! Therefore, I will do according to your word. I will give you a wise and discerning mind so that there has never been nor shall there ever be one like you in all the world. I will also give you what you did not ask, riches and honor."

When Solomon awoke, he realized God had come to him in a dream.

"Reverence for the Lord," Solomon taught his people, "is the foundation of knowledge, but fools despise wisdom and instruction."

Solomon did not keep his wisdom to himself. It was a gift from God that he yearned to share with all the people of Israel, a gift that he hoped would last long after his death. So he began to compile his insights into a book, into the book called Proverbs.

Throughout his life Solomon added to this book, carefully recording new understandings that God granted him.

Israel enjoyed uninterrupted peace during Solomon's reign, so Solomon was able to do something that David had only dreamed of. He built a magnificent temple to honor the Lord. In return, God promised Solomon, "If you and your sons live obediently and serve me only, doing all that I have commanded and never turning aside to worship other gods, then your sons shall reign forever on David's throne."

For many years Solomon served God faithfully, but eventually his faith grew cold. The Lord had appeared to Solomon twice, commanding him not to worship other gods, yet Solomon did just that.

Throughout his reign Solomon had married many foreign women. They brought into Israel, into Jerusalem, and into his own house their foreign gods. And when the king was an old man, his love for his wives overshadowed his love for the Lord. A part of his heart went to the goddess Ashtoreth, a part of his heart to Milcom, a part to Chemosh, a part to Molech. Solomon even built temples for these last two gods. Solomon's heart was not true to the Lord God.

A third time, God spoke to Solomon. "Not in your lifetime," he said, "but soon after your death, Solomon, I will tear the kingdom from your throne. However, for the sake of my servant David, one tribe alone shall be left unto your son. Judah and Jerusalem alone shall be his."

And so it was.

After Solomon died, the northern tribes of Israel all rebelled against his son Rehoboam.

Since Rehoboam was not as shrewd as his father Solomon nor as courageous as his grandfather David; since he was a weak, arrogant, and childish king, the northern tribes succeeded in their rebellion against him. They set up a new kingdom with a new king. And so there was a tear in the fabric of Israel, a split in the family that had, in times before, lived as one.

The northern kingdom called itself Israel; the southern, Judah. The Lord still was God for both of them, but God's children no longer loved one another as once they had. God's people no longer served God as they once had.

Prophet Versus King

Especially in the northern kingdom of Israel, the kings and people welcomed the false god Baal. Especially there, Baal worship grew like a cancer in the souls of the people. Yet even in Judah people made room for other gods.

But God—who grieved to see his people turn away—the Lord God did not cease to love them!

"What shall I do with you, Israel?" he said. "Judah, what

shall I do with you? Your love is like the morning cloud, like the dew that goes early away!"

What the Lord did was this: He kept speaking his word even now unto his people! The same word that he had spoken from the beginning. But now it was not Moses, nor Joshua, nor the judges, nor the priests, nor the kings who carried that word for the Lord. It was the prophets!

The prophets. Individuals who loved God mightily, who agonized over the sin of the people, and who cried God's word unto them. The prophets...

Now the seventh king of the northern kingdom did evil in the sight of the Lord. Indeed, more than all the kings who went before, he defied God's laws and rejected God.

So Elijah the prophet went to the king's palace and demanded an audience with King Ahab.

"As the Lord God lives," said Elijah, "the Lord whom I serve, there shall be neither dew nor rain these years—until my word calls them back again."

And so it was that the land became dry, baked like a brick in an oven. For three years the drought burned the land.

One day Ahab himself went out searching for grass to feed his horses. He found no grass, but he did encounter Elijah— the source of his trouble!

Calmly, Elijah confronted Ahab for his worship of Baal. Then the prophet Elijah challenged King Ahab to a public contest between Baal's 450 prophets and Elijah, between Baal and the Lord.

When everyone had gathered on Mount Carmel, Elijah spoke to the people. "Choose one or the other!" he cried. "If the Lord is God, follow him, but if Baal is God, follow him."

Then Elijah turned to Baal's prophets, "Have two bulls brought. You choose one; then cut it to pieces, lay it on wood, but put no fire to it. I will take the other bull and do the same. You call on your god; I will call upon the Lord. The god who answers by fire—he is God!"

The contest was on! From morning until midafternoon, the 450 prophets of Baal pleaded with their god to send down fire. But Baal didn't answer. Baal didn't act. Slowly, carefully Elijah arranged the wood on a stone altar. Then, when the sacrifice was ready, he had four huge jars of water poured over it—once, twice, a third time! Twelve jars for the twelve tribes of Israel.

"Now, O Lord, God of Abraham, Isaac, and Israel," Elijah prayed, "show that you are God in Israel, that I am your servant, and that I have done all these things at your command. Answer me, Lord God, answer me—that your people may know that you are indeed God."

Suddenly the fire of the Lord fell, consuming the meat, the wood, the stones, the dust—even licking the water up from around the trench.

The people fell down on their faces and shouted, "The Lord, he is God! The Lord, he is God!" Israel had returned to their God!

Unfortunately, the people were nearly as quick to abandon their God once again.

1 KINGS 18

Israel and Judah Exiled

Throughout the years that followed, God continued to send prophets with messages of rebuke and warning, seeking to bring his people back to him. But the prophets had little lasting effect.

Jonah, who spent three days and nights in the belly of a large fish learning obedience to God; Amos, who left his life as a farmer to challenge Israel's religious leaders; Hosea, whose marriage to a prostitute symbolized God's relationship to Israel; Isaiah, who both warned of judgment and promised a coming Messiah—these and many others offered the people of Israel mercy if only they would repent and return to the Lord. But still the kings and the people ignored the Lord.

Israel, the northern kingdom, was the worst—and the first to fall. With an army terrifying and swift, the Assyrians swept through the promised land and carried the Israelites away to the east. They would never return. The exile had begun.

Judah, the kingdom to the south, enjoyed a short reprieve. Two of its kings, Hezekiah and Josiah, pleased God and brought the people closer to him. However, all hope for lasting reform died with Josiah, the last good king to sit on David's throne. God's judgment was just over the eastern horizon.

Babylon was the latest in a series of powerful empires. The Babylonians had already swallowed up mighty Assyria, but they were hungry for more land and tribute. Their king, Nebuchadnezzar, had Judah squarely in his sights.

So he led his armies into Judah and captured every fortified city. He plundered Jerusalem, taking many leading citizens and much wealth. He even took the gold and silver utensils from the Temple. A decade later, when the people he left behind rebelled, he returned and burned everything—the city, the walls, the palace, the Temple. Then Nebuchadnezzar took the people of Judah into exile in Babylon.

The prophet Jeremiah had for many years tried to turn people's hearts, but they had not listened. Now, he continued to speak God's message, but this time it was a message of hope.

" 'Behold, days are coming,' says the Lord, 'when I will make a new covenant with the house of Israel and the house of Judah, not like the old one that I made with their fathers when I brought them out of Egypt, my covenant that they broke. This is the new covenant: I will put my law within them. I will write it upon their hearts. I will be their God, and they shall be my people. They shall all know me, for I will forgive their evil deeds and remember their sin no more.' "

So spoke Jeremiah words of comfort even in the days of weeping. Then he added, "Judah shall come back from the land of the enemy, from the land of Babylon. 'There is hope for the future,' says the Lord."

Daniel in the Lions' Den

When Nebuchadnezzar brought the best of Judah to Babylon—the nobility, the priests, the educated, the wealthy—he wanted the best of the best for himself.

"I want," he commanded his servant, "boys both handsome and intelligent, boys skillful and ready to learn. Raise them in my palace; educate them, and, at the end of three years, they will serve me."

So his servant searched and found the best. Among them was Daniel.

Daniel served in Nebuchadnezzar's government for many years. When Daniel was much older, a new power arose, and Darius of the Medes overthrew the Babylonians. Soon Daniel became an official in the new government. Darius recognized talent when he saw it.

Daniel was filled with such wisdom that the king planned to set him over the entire kingdom. So the provincial governors and palace administrators jealously hated him and looked for some fault that would discredit him in Darius' eyes.

But Daniel was faithful. No fault was found in the man.

Therefore, they conceived a plan by which to break him and to bring him down.

"King," they said to Darius, "we have discussed the matter together, and we believe that you are equal to any god."

Darius smiled.

"Therefore, make a law that, for the next thirty days, anyone who worships another god besides yourself shall be cast into the den of lions."

Darius mused, smiled, and nodded.

"Good! Here is the law written out, O King," they said. "Sign it so that it cannot be changed."

Darius signed the law. It could not be changed.

With victory close at hand, the governors and administrators went as a group and hid outside of Daniel's window.

Although Daniel knew of the law, he never once broke his custom. Daily, three times a day, he kneeled at a window open to Jerusalem, praying and giving thanks to the Lord his God. No law, not even that of the Medes and the Persians, would break his faithfulness to God.

"Aha!" cried the men. "This man of Judah sneers at the law of the king of the Medes!" So they returned to Darius to lodge their accusation.

"King," one of them asked, "didn't you sign a law that no one could worship any god but you?"

"I did," Darius replied.

"And wasn't the punishment that such a one be cast into the lions' den?"

"It was," said Darius, "and it still is so. I signed it. It cannot be changed."

"I thought so," said the official. "That Daniel, that fellow from Judah, ignores your law. Three times a day he prays to his own god!"

The king, when he heard this, was distressed. The whole day through, until the sun went down, he tried to think of ways to rescue Daniel.

But the officials kept reminding him, "You signed the law. It cannot be changed."

Finally Darius muttered the command, and Daniel was cast into the den of lions. It was a pit with a narrow hole at the top, a wide floor at the bottom, and lions. And Daniel.

"May your God deliver you," said Darius as a stone was pushed over the opening. "May your God, dear Daniel, deliver you," as he sealed the stone with his own ring. Then the king went to his palace, where he spent the night restless, unable to eat or to sleep.

At the break of day, Darius ran back to the den. Anguish in his voice, he cried, "Daniel! Daniel! Daniel! Has your God been able to deliver you from the lions?"

Then Daniel, from the hollow of the pit, answered, "King, my God sent his angel to shut the lions' mouths. Because I am blameless before him, they have not hurt me."

Darius smiled with relief—and ordered those who had accused Daniel to try a night for themselves in the den of lions. And then he decreed that everyone serve and reverence the God of Daniel, the God of Israel.

Going Home Again!

Seventy years God's people were in Babylon, seventy years bowed down under the rule of foreign kings in foreign lands. But God had promised that they would return home...

A buzzing in homes of the Jews. Exiles whispering in one another's ears. The raising of grateful hands to heaven. The exiles have heard the message. God is at work in the hearts of the peoples! God has moved the king of the vast Persian empire to make a decree. The decree is law; it cannot be changed. For thus says Cyrus, king of Persia:

"The Lord, the God of heaven, charged me to build him a temple in Jerusalem, which is in Judah. Therefore, let all his people return to Jerusalem and rebuild the house of the Lord, the God of Israel. Let the cost be paid from the royal treasury, and let the gold and silver vessels, which Nebuchadnezzar took from the house of God, be taken back to the Temple, each to its proper place!"

Now there is hasty labor and happy preparation in the homes of the Jews. Fathers gather their families together. The priests, the Levites, and the Temple servants assemble as one. Jews who had been held captive in Babylon gather in a great assembly... and go home.

Three months after the people had returned, when they had settled in their towns and homes again, they all gathered as one in Jerusalem. Near the ruined, gutted house of God they built the altar of the God of Israel, and there they began again to offer their burnt offerings to the Lord. Daily, morning and evening, according to the laws, they offered sacrifices and kept all the appointed feasts of the Lord.

And when the Temple was finally completed, they gathered with a holy and a careful joy. They sacrificed hundreds of lambs, rams, and bulls to the Lord, goats as sin offerings for each of the twelve tribes. Then they celebrated the Passover in memory of all the merciful acts the Lord had done to save them throughout their history.

Joy burst the hearts of the Jews. Tears overflowed their eyes. For the Lord had made them glad again—the Lord, the God of Israel!

Jerusalem, when the people returned to it, was without a

wall. As long as the wall was a crumbled ruin, the enemies of
the Jews were happy. Jerusalem posed no threat to them. They
could, if they wished, simply march into the city and harass it
with a sword and a little knife.

Then the leaders of the Jews said, "Let's rebuild the wall!"

The work began . . . and the enemies of the Jews were no
longer happy.

At first they sneered at the labor. "What are these feeble
Jews doing?" they said. "Ha! Even a fox could knock through
such a wall."

But the work went on.

And on the fifty-second day, it was done.

Then all the people of Judah assembled within the walled
city, Jerusalem. Early in the morning a man named Ezra
stepped out in front of them. He climbed a wooden platform,
so that he might be seen by everyone, and opened a scroll.
When he opened the scroll, all of the people stood and waited.

Ezra began to read from the scroll. Clearly, in a ringing
voice, in familiar language, Ezra read. All the people listened
intently. Then the Torah—God's law—was explained so that
everyone understood it.

And when they heard the ancient teachings, when the
people understood, they wept. They confessed their sins—
theirs and the sins of all their ancestors.

But Ezra comforted the people, saying, "This day is holy to
the Lord your God. Do not mourn or weep. Do not be grieved, for the joy of the Lord is your strength!"

By his gentle directing, the people changed. Tears turned

to joy, sorrow into thanksgiving. Day by day Ezra read from the scroll of the Torah. And when the people heard his reading, there was great rejoicing.

God had spoken to his people once again. Through Israel's long history, its steady growth from a family to a people to a nation, the Lord had always spoken to his people. Through his laws, his priests, his kings, and his prophets, God had always spoken the right word at exactly the right time.

But God wasn't finished. The best was yet to come. God was about to speak to his people, to all people, face to face.

Jesus, the Word of God

In the beginning was the Word.
    The Word was with God,
    and the Word was God.
He was with God in the beginning.

All things were made through him—
    not one thing made that he did not make!
Life itself was in the Word,
    and this life was the light of all people,
    and this light still shines in the darkness,
    for the darkness has not overcome it!

The Word was in the world,
    the world that was made through him,
    yet the world refused to know him.

The Word came to his own people,
    yet his people refused to receive him.

But to those who received him,
    to those who believed in him,
    he gave power to make them children of God!

Yes, the Word of God became flesh
    and lived among us,
    blazing with grace and truth!

The story of Jesus, the Word, begins with Abraham. The story of the family of Israel continues when Jesus appears. There are, after all, not two stories, but one—the whole of the Bible, the Old and the New Testaments together.

Angelic Visitations

North of Jerusalem, where the Temple was; north of the whole territory of Judea, in which Jerusalem was; north even of the territory of Samaria; in the province of Galilee, in a small town of that province, in Nazareth, there lived a young woman whose life was gentle, kind, and unassuming and whose single expectation was that she would one day marry the man to whom she was engaged.

But God would change that. This woman's family would contain a most uncommon wonder—beyond all expectations! By this young woman every family in every nation could anticipate extraordinary blessings, for through this ordinary woman God himself was about to do a new thing.

The man to whom she was engaged was Joseph, the son of Jacob, of the house of David. He was a carpenter. The woman's name was Mary. She was a virgin.

One day the angel of the Lord appeared unto Mary, flooding her little house with light.

"Greetings, God's favored one! The Lord is with you!"

Young Mary trembled, wondering what sort of greeting this was.

But the angel said to her, "Don't be afraid, Mary. You have indeed found favor with God. Listen—you are going to become pregnant, and you will bear a son whose name you shall call Jesus. Your son will be great. He will be called the Son of the Most High. The Lord God will establish him on the throne of his father David, and he will reign over the people of Israel forever. Forever! To his kingdom there will be no end!"

"How . . . ?" Mary began, but then she hesitated. Oh, these were grand pronouncements from the bright and shining messenger of God, and she could dearly believe them. But one small, utterly common fact seemed overlooked, something so obvious—

"How can this be?" she asked. "I'm not married yet. I'm a virgin."

"The Holy Spirit will come upon you," announced the angel, "and the power of the Most High will overshadow you. Therefore, the child to be born of you will be called holy, the Son of God. Mary, with God nothing is impossible. Even your relative Elizabeth, whom everyone called barren and who should have been too old for children, even she is now with child."

Mary smiled. "I am the servant of my Lord," she said. "Let it be for me according to your words."

Then the angel departed, leaving Mary alone in her house.

Soon after the angel had gone, Mary left Nazareth and rushed off to visit her relative. "Elizabeth! Elizabeth!" she cried. "Do you know what has happened to me?" Elizabeth gasped, felt her side for an instant, and threw her arms around Mary.

"Oh, blessed are you among women!" she cried. Elizabeth knew, for in her womb was the one people would call John the Baptist, the one promised to prepare the way for the Lord's Messiah. And the child in Elizabeth's womb had leaped for joy when he heard Mary's voice.

Mary could not restrain her excitement. "Elizabeth, my soul exalts the Lord! My spirit rejoices in God my Savior! He has done great things for me, and I will be called blessed by all people from this day on!"

Mary stayed with Elizabeth for about three months, then returned to her home in Nazareth.

Mary and Joseph were not yet married, nor did they live together. But they were engaged to each other, and in those days that was a very solemn thing. It meant that they had promised their lives to each other, their hearts, their bodies, and all their days. They had made this promise before God and in the presence of their families, and now they were waiting for the wedding day—when Mary would move into Joseph's house as his wife.

Joseph was a good man, stable, honorable, dependable,

and, like Mary, both quiet and devout. Joseph was a good man. He did not mind that Mary went alone to visit Elizabeth. Neither did he mind that she was three months gone from him. Nor did he complain, when she returned, that she had changed somewhat, being a little more given to tears and much more secretive. He did not ask her what her secret was.

But when her secret began to tell itself and it became evident that she was pregnant, then the good man became a sad man, for it seemed that Mary had broken her promise to him. Joseph thought long and decided that there was really no alternative but to divorce her. Tomorrow.

But Joseph was a good, just man. He had the legal right to shame Mary for her sin before all the people, but he hated the thought of Mary in humiliation. So Joseph determined, rather, to divorce her quietly. Two witnesses and a piece of paper were all that he would need. Two witnesses and a piece of paper, and that would be the end to it. Tomorrow. He would do the deed tomorrow.

It was a fitful sleep that Joseph slept that night. It was also a divine sleep, for an angel came into it, and his dreams were filled with the light of the messenger from God.

"Joseph, son of David!" called the angel. The good man, even in his sleep, listened with a sincere faith.

"What, my lord?"

"Do not be afraid to take Mary as your wife, for the child in her is of no sin. He is of the Holy Spirit. Mary will bear her son, and you, Joseph, shall call his name Jesus—because he will save his people from their sins."

There was no divorce on the morrow, no shame nor any sorrow. God was fulfilling what he had promised so long ago through the prophet Isaiah.

"A virgin shall conceive and bear a son, and his name shall be called Immanuel." In Hebrew, Immanuel means "God with us."

Now was the right time! Now was the Lord God keeping that promise! The virgin about to bear a son was Mary, and, although her son's given name would be Jesus, his whole being would be Immanuel: God with us!

The Birth of Jesus

Now the birth of Jesus happened this way.

Caesar Augustus, emperor of the entire Roman Empire, commanded a counting of all his people.

"Count them by families!" the order went out. "Count them in the cities of their ancestors. Record the count that we may tax every one of them!"

So it was ordered. So it was done.

All over the world people began to travel this way and that, short distances and long, to the homes of their heritage. In Spain on the west, in Gaul, in the deserts of northern Africa, as far east as the Euphrates, even in little Nazareth of Galilee, the people bagged their belongings and traveled.

One good man also obeyed the order, though his wife, being in the ninth month of her pregnancy, was in no condition to travel. By slow stages Joseph and Mary moved south from

Galilee, into Judea and past the city of Jerusalem. They continued south until they came to the tiny town of Bethlehem, the ancestral city of David. There they meant to stay.

But it was late, and the town was full of the family of David. The inn had no rooms available; the rooms had no beds unoccupied. But the birth pains were hurting poor Mary, so Joseph searched frantically for some shelter, some soft place where she might bear her baby.

There was so little time.

Finally Joseph returned and announced, "I found a place." Then he led Mary around to the back of an inn, where there was a low stone fence and a rough thatched roof against the wall. Here, in this lean-to, the innkeeper shut up animals for the night. Here Joseph meant to lodge his Mary for the night. But Mary asked no questions. There was no time.

She shaped a little bed in straw, then leaned into her labor and strained for dear life.

Mary delivered her baby—a son. She washed him and wound him in strips of cloth; then with mother's hands, somewhat swollen and tired, but infinitely gentle, she laid him in a feeding trough.

In the darkness of the night, a distant dog barked and kept on barking. It must have been a private matter between him and the stars, for no one else was disturbed. The shepherds' own guard dog raised his head once and perked his ears, then lay down again. The sheep were sleeping. The fields near Bethlehem were still—dark outlines against a starry sky; all signs of peace. The shepherds were concerned only to keep awake and to keep watch over their flocks until morning.

They were lying on the ground, leaning on their elbows, and talking of common, forgettable things...

Suddenly the entire night sky blazed with a furious light. The glory of God shone all around them, and an angel stepped forward. The animals were stunned cold; the shepherds threw up their arms in fear and shouted, "Ahhhhh!"

"No, don't be afraid," pleaded the angel, but none of the shepherds lowered his arms.

"Good news!" said the angel. "Listen, I'm bringing you good news of great joy, and joy it shall be for all people! For to you is born this day, in the city of David, a Savior who is Christ the Lord! Now, this shall be a sign for you..."

Two of the shepherds lowered their arms the better to listen. A sign! They would want a sign to ratify such news as this and such a vision!

"You will find the infant wrapped in strips of cloth and lying in a feeding trough."

All at once the deep sky was filled with angels—as many as there had been stars before. They were praising God in a thrilling voice, saying, "Glory to God in the highest; peace to the people with whom he is pleased!"

Then the angels returned into heaven, and the chorus was over. The chill stars shone like ice again, and the night was vastly dark.

There was a moment of absolute silence among the

shepherds—until one man whispered, "Did you...?"

"I did! I saw it!" said another.

"Angels and good news!" cried a third.

"And a sign!"

Then the shepherds, every single one of them, threw back their heads and burst into long, loud, and joyful laughter. A little band of men under the infinite sky, they nudged one another and slapped their knees and laughed until the tears rolled down their cheeks—and the sheep blinked at them.

"Why not?" roared the shepherds. "Why shouldn't we go to Bethlehem to see what the angel told us about?"

And when their happy laughter had settled somewhat, they did.

They found the feeding trough. They found Mary and Joseph. And they found the newborn child, whom the angel had called Christ the Lord.

Again they started laughing. But this time they woke people with their laughter. They told everyone who would listen what the angel had said about the child, and the people were amazed. Then they went back to their sheep in the dawning light, but they did not stop glorifying God and praising him for all that they had heard and seen.

Mary, who had borne the child; Mary, who had watched the shepherds come, who understood the source of their raucous laughter, and who had seen them go; Mary picked up the child and closed her eyes. Even so did she keep these things as a treasure in her heart and remember them.

LUKE 2

Herod and the Wise Men

At that time the king of Judea was an old, embittered, and suspicious man named Herod—a cunning man and a man quite willing to murder in order to keep his crown. However, Herod the Great was not long for the world, for death sat on his shoulders. Herod was sick with a killing illness, but that did not soften him. Instead, it made him desperate and sharpened his wickedness. Beware old men who do not want to die!

One day, many months after Jesus' birth, wise men from the East, wise men who watched the stars, came to Jerusalem looking for a new king. Old Herod was not pleased. "Here I am!" he snapped. But they were looking for one newly born king of the Jews. "We saw his star when it rose, and we have come to worship him," they said.

"The Messiah!" Herod suddenly realized who they must be talking about. Then secretly he conceived an evil plan. He had his scribes look up where the Messiah, who was to save the people of Israel, was to be born.

"Bethlehem," he reported to the wise men. "You'll find him in Bethlehem. When you find him, please report to me exactly where he is so that I can worship him too." But worship wasn't exactly what Herod had in mind.

With what high dignity these foreigners entered the house of Jesus the King. Mary, his mother, received them, but to Jesus himself went their worship and their gifts. They knelt before him, and they opened unto him their treasures: gold, incense, and myrrh.

Then the same God who had blessed them with a star blessed them again with a warning. He told them not to return to Herod—ever. So they returned to their own land by another route.

Joseph, too, had been given a warning: to leave Bethlehem and Judea at once, to take both Mary and Jesus as far away as Egypt, and to live there until it was safe to return. Joseph obeyed, and the little family fled by night.

A week passed, then two, then a month. Still no wise men. Eventually Herod realized that they weren't coming back. Enraged by the wise men's deception, Herod gave orders to kill all the boys in Bethlehem and its vicinity who were two years old and under!

But Herod did not live much longer than these children. The disease in the old man's mind and body took his rage, his crown, and his life.

Then Joseph felt free to bring his family back to the land of Israel. But because Herod's son began to rule in Judea, they never returned to Bethlehem. They went all the way home again to Nazareth in Galilee, and there they raised the child.

In His Father's House

Jesus grew, over the years, into a fine, strong boy—wiser than mortals are wise and full of the favor of God.

Sometimes even his parents were astonished by his insight and understanding. Once, when he was twelve years old, his parents took him to Jerusalem to celebrate the Passover. Eight days they spent among the crowds, worshiping God and remembering his saving deeds. Then, at the end of the Feast, Mary and Joseph began the long journey home, walking with their friends from Nazareth, supposing that Jesus was with others, walking in the same direction.

That night they looked for him...but found him nowhere in the group.

"Did you see him?" they asked his friends. But no one had seen him.

"Didn't he come at all?" they wondered. Slowly, fearfully they admitted that no, he had not come. They had left him behind!

Immediately Mary and Joseph turned around and walked alone all the way back to Jerusalem. For three days they searched and worried and blamed themselves for not taking better care of their son.

They found him, finally, in the Temple, sitting quite happily among the teachers, listening and asking questions, speaking with such wisdom that everyone was astonished.

Suddenly Mary interrupted the scholarly conversation. "Son!" she scolded him. "How could you do this to us? Don't you know that your father and I have been worried, looking everywhere for you?"

"Why were you looking for me?" Jesus asked her. "Didn't you know that I must be in my Father's house?"

Neither of his parents understood these words. But Mary, when they had returned to Nazareth, Mary would sometimes close her eyes, think of an evening long past, and remember in silence all the words and the deeds that concerned her son.

During the years that followed, Jesus grew in wisdom, in stature, and in favor with God and all of the people. Then came Jesus to Israel, preaching the good news that God's kingdom—God's rule—was close at hand.

God filled Jesus of Nazareth with the Holy Spirit and with power. Then Jesus went about doing good and healing all who were oppressed by the devil, for God was with Jesus.

This ministry to all people began when Jesus was a young man of about thirty.

John Prepares the Way

It was in the fifteenth year of the reign of the Roman emperor Tiberius, when Pontius Pilate was the governor of Judea, that God spoke to John, the son of Elizabeth and Zechariah. Then John, who had been waiting in the wilderness, began like the storm of God to preach.

"Repent!" he cried.

His voice echoed in the wilderness, then resounded through the villages, towns, and cities of Judea. Everyone heard, and crowds went out to him.

They found a bold and eloquent, compelling man. A prophet! His clothes were made of camel's hair. He wore a wide leather belt about his waist. He ate locusts and wild honey. For all that, it was not what the man wore but what the man said that drew the people to him. It was what John the Baptizer said and did for God's people.

"Repent!" he cried. "For the kingdom of heaven is not far

away. God's rule is close at hand!" With drilling, transforming words he told people to repent from their sins, to accept God's forgiveness, to be baptized as a sign of their changed hearts. Then, in the Jordan River, he baptized a repentant people.

So he preached; so he baptized. And his reputation swept like a searing wind across the countryside.

The religious leaders in Jerusalem began to hear rumblings about John, so they sent a delegation to ask who he was.

"In the words of Isaiah," replied John, "I am 'the voice of one crying in the wilderness, the one preparing the way for the Lord!' "

"I baptize you with water," he continued, "but there stands among you one whom you do not know, one so much mightier than I that I am unworthy to untie his sandals. He will baptize you with the Holy Spirit."

Jesus stepped forward to be baptized. John knew that Jesus didn't need to be cleansed from sins, so at first John refused. But Jesus insisted that John baptize him, and so he did.

Immediately, when Jesus came up from the water, the heavens split open and the Spirit of God descended upon him in the form of a dove. Then a voice from heaven declared, "This is my beloved Son. With him I am well pleased!"

Still wet, Jesus draped his tunic over his shoulders, turned, and walked into the desert without a word. The Spirit was pressing him to leave. Jesus was being driven to be utterly alone, to make himself vulnerable in the dry, dead wilderness.

Forty days and nights he wandered, never eating. The wind howled. Jesus grew hungry. His stomach shriveled, shrank, and hardened. Then, at the end of that time, the devil came to him.

He came to tempt Jesus to sin. Three times he tried. Three times he failed. Three times Jesus rejected Satan's tempting offers by quoting Scripture. Finally the devil departed in defeat, leaving Jesus alone.

Then angels came to comfort him and to attend to his needs.

When John saw Jesus once again on the east side of the Jordan, he raised a finger, pointed, and cried the truth to the crowd, "Pay attention! Look! Do you see that man?"

There stood a quiet, intense young man gazing straight into John's eyes, thin from the ordeal he had just endured, but in perfect control of himself and of the situation.

"He," cried John, "is the Lamb of God who takes away the sin of the world! His ministry follows mine, but he himself was ever before me. I saw the Spirit of God descend upon him as a dove from heaven. I have seen, and I bear witness to you that this is the Son of God!"

Jesus' Ministry Begins

Quietly Jesus walked into Galilee. With no great acclaim, he returned to the towns of his youth. Almost no one understood who he was or what he was about to do.

A wedding feast. A common affair. A happy and joyful occasion. Late in the evening, Jesus watched the proud bridegroom march through the streets of Cana to the house of his bride. When they returned together through the same streets to the groom's house, Jesus quietly joined the procession.

At the groom's house, a feast was found ready for the eating. The guests began to eat, to drink, to tell stories, to enjoy themselves. A wedding feast. A common and good celebration.

But something happened here in Cana to make it both uncommon and miraculous.

"There is a problem," Jesus' mother said to him. "They have run out of wine."

Jesus gazed at his mother for a moment. "And what does that have to do with me?" he asked.

She laid her finger by her cheek, as if to say, "But I know you. I know."

"My time has not yet come," Jesus explained.

Mary said nothing more to him. Instead, she went to the servants and pointed toward Jesus.

"Do whatever that man asks you to do," she instructed.

There were six stone jars standing in the courtyard, each jar large enough to hold at least twenty gallons. Jesus arose, looked at the jars, and found them empty. Then to the servants he said, "Fill these jars with water."

They did. They filled them to the brim.

When that was done, Jesus said, "Now, take a cupful to the master of ceremonies and ask him to taste of it."

One servant dipped a cup into one stone jar and carried it to the man in charge of the feast. He tasted it and declared approvingly that the cup held an excellent wine.

Turning to the groom, he asked, "Why did you do this? Everyone else serves the good wine first and then, after it's gone, the poor wine. But you saved the best for now!"

The groom had no answer, but the servants knew that the groom had nothing to do with it. They knew, rather, that this was a miracle. Jesus would perform many more, and many people would put their trust in him because of the miracles.

Then it was that Jesus ceased to be quiet. He went out into the towns and villages of Galilee. He opened up his mouth, and with a sudden, blazing authority he began to preach.

"The time is fulfilled!" he cried in the markets, he cried in the synagogues, he preached in the streets and the houses. "It is ready to happen! The kingdom of God is at hand. Israel! Repent and believe in the good news!"

The people came out and listened to him, for his preaching was a bright, glorious thing. It seemed to them like a light shining into the deep gloom of their lives. They had been sighing in darkness, but here, standing before this Jesus, they were waking to the morning!

So the word spread about Jesus.

"He preaches with power and authority," they said. "There is truth in his words!"

From every direction, the hungry people flocked to feed on his words, to stand in his love, and to receive blessing from his hands. Wherever he went, crowds of needy people appeared, for his ministry was not only in words but also in deeds.

He gave sight to the blind, hearing to the deaf, freedom to the demon-oppressed. And so it was that in a very short time the crowds grew. The ministry had begun.

Jesus Calls Four Fishermen

One day Jesus went to the city of Capernaum, which is on the Sea of Galilee. He preached on the shores of that sea, and the crowds were there in such numbers that he could not be heard.

But he saw two fishing boats beached nearby and fishers cleaning their nets after fishing the long night through.

Jesus spoke to one of them, a muscular, thickset man whose gestures were both impressive and impatient. "Simon," he said.

"What?" Simon whirled around, ready to argue with anyone. He was in a foul mood, having caught no fish the night before. But Jesus had kind, level eyes, and the fight went out of Simon. "What is it?" he asked.

"Would you row me away from the shore? I have something to say to the people."

Simon looked at the waiting crowds and then at the lean man whom the crowds had come to hear. The fisherman shrugged. "Why not?"

So the people sat down on the banks, which rose from the water like a natural theater, and Jesus talked to them from Simon's boat. Simon had little choice but to listen too.

When Jesus was done speaking, Simon took the oars, preparing to row his passenger back to land.

"No," said Jesus. "I would rather that you row out to deeper water."

"What? Why?" asked Simon impatiently. "What's out there for you?"

MATTHEW 4; LUKE 5

"Not for me, but for you," said Jesus as mildly as the breeze. "Let down your nets, and you will find fish."

"Look, sir," replied Simon, "I am the fisherman in this boat, and I am the fisherman of this boat. I don't mean to offend you, but I know that the day is no time for fishing— and this day in particular because we took absolutely nothing last night. Now, if I have done enough for you . . . "

"Simon!" said Jesus.

"What!" said Simon.

"Do it."

And, in spite of his conviction that this was all a ridiculous waste of time, Simon did as Jesus commanded.

Suddenly Simon became amazed, then mortified. His nets held so many fish that they began to break.

"John! John!" he roared. "James! Andrew, help me!"

A second boat rushed out to help with the fish, but even two were too few, and they began to sink under the heavy load.

The burly fisherman looked at Jesus with new eyes. He was frightened to discover who truly sat in his boat with him, and he knelt at Jesus' feet. "O Lord, go away from me," he pleaded. "I am a sinful man!"

But Jesus, as gentle as the wind, touched him on his head and said, "No, Simon, don't be afraid. From this time forward you will be catching people and not fish. Follow me."

So it was that when they brought their boats to land, Simon and his brother Andrew, James and his brother John left everything that they owned to follow Jesus.

"You, Simon," said Jesus to the vigorous fisherman, "I will call you Peter." Peter—the "rock"!

Thus Jesus began to choose certain individuals to follow him more closely than the curious crowds. These walked with him, ate with him, laughed with him, and learned from him—they were called his disciples.

Besides the four fishermen, there was Philip, who also brought Bartholomew to Jesus. There was Matthew, who had been a tax collector before Jesus called him from his tables. There were Thomas; James, the son of Alphaeus; Simon, who was called the Zealot; and Judas, the son of James. Finally there was Judas Iscariot, who would one day betray Jesus.

Twelve in all.

Mixed Reviews

Wherever they learned of Jesus' presence, distressed and oppressed people would come begging him, "Jesus! Oh, Jesus, please help us!" Then Jesus would turn a penetrating eye upon them—and help them far beyond their poor imaginings.

Once, when Jesus entered the house of Simon Peter, he found everything hushed. All was whispers and darkness and walking on tiptoe. Peter himself came out of a side room with a look of grave concern and wide-eyed fear. When he saw Jesus, he shook his head.

"My mother-in-law," he whispered. "She's suffering from a violent fever."

Jesus nodded in understanding, then went into the room

Peter had just left. He found the woman lying in bed, dry and hot and breathing with rapid gasps. Jesus gazed at her for a moment, then took her hand and lifted her up. At his touch alone, the fever broke and left her, and the woman was well.

Then the house was filled with happier sounds, laughter and excited chatter. In fact, the woman felt so good that she came out and served everyone dinner.

Unfortunately, the crowds that surrounded Jesus were not all kindly, not all needy, not all faithful people seeking to believe in him.

Here and there suspicious faces appeared among the others. Some were scribes, the scholars of the law; some were Pharisees, who made a practice of keeping not only the written law of Moses but also all the laws passed down by word of mouth from the teachers of previous generations. "If you strive to keep the little laws," they taught, "you will never break the big ones."

They came to catch this teacher breaking any law, little or big, written or unwritten.

When Jesus looked out and saw these faces among the sick and the sorrowing, he was grieved by the hardness of the people's hearts, for they looked like stones in a plowed field.

On a certain Sabbath day, Jesus noticed a man whose hand was shriveled and, beside him, a Pharisee. Both stood amidst the crowd that always followed after Jesus.

He said to the man with the gnarled hand, "Come here."

While that man came forward, the eyes of the Pharisee

grew narrow with thought. If Jesus heals the man, he thought, he will have worked on the Sabbath. And if he works, he breaks the Sabbath law that forbids any work.

As always, Jesus knew what the Pharisee was thinking.

"Let me ask you something," he said to the Pharisee.

"Me?" The Pharisee was startled.

"You." Jesus took the withered hand into his own. "Is it lawful on the Sabbath to do good or to do harm?"

No answer from the Pharisee. He seemed to be deep in thought.

"If you have a sheep that falls into a ditch on the Sabbath day," said Jesus in a sharper voice, "will you not rescue that sheep—on the Sabbath day?"

No answer from the Pharisee.

Jesus held high the poor, withered hand. "But a person," he said in a voice clearly angry, "a person is more valuable than a sheep! Have you never learned that the Sabbath was made for humans—for humans!—and not the other way around?"

Still no answer from the Pharisee, though a turmoil of thought now raced through his mind.

Jesus turned back to the man beside him and spoke words suddenly gentle and kind. "Stretch out your hand," he said.

The man withdrew his hand from Jesus, held it out in front of him, and moved it easily. The hand was completely healed.

In the commotion that followed, the Pharisee and his friends slipped away. They began immediately to consider how they might discredit Jesus, destroy Jesus.

Jesus' Sermon on the Mount

Out of the city Jesus went with his disciples—not only with the Twelve but with all those who dearly sought the kingdom of God. He led them through the countryside and up a mountain. Finally he sat down, and his disciples gathered around him.

Then Jesus taught them, saying,

"Blessed are those who admit their spiritual neediness, for theirs is the kingdom of heaven.

"Blessed are those who mourn, for they shall be comforted.

"Blessed are the meek, for they shall inherit the earth.

"Blessed are those who hunger and thirst for righteousness, for they shall be filled.

"Blessed are the merciful, for they shall obtain mercy.

"Blessed are the pure in heart, for they shall see God.

"Blessed are the peacemakers, for they shall be called the children of God.

"Blessed are those who are persecuted for the sake of righteousness, for theirs is the kingdom of heaven.

"Blessed are you when the world mocks you, hurts you, speaks every evil against you falsely because of me. Rejoice, my disciples, and be glad when that happens, for your reward in heaven will be great. In the same way they mocked the prophets who went before you.

"You!" Jesus said unto them. He gazed into their eyes, one disciple after the other. "You are the salt of the earth. But if the salt has lost its taste, can it ever be salty again?

No, then it is good for nothing but to be thrown on the ground and trampled underfoot.

"You!" he said, as though it were the given name of every one of them. "You are the light of the world. But a candle kept under a basket brightens nothing. However, a candle on a stand gives light to all the house. Let your light so shine before people that they may see your good works and give glory to your Father who is in heaven.

"You, my disciples; you, salt of the earth and light of the world—be perfect as your Father in heaven is perfect."

"When you pray," he continued, "do not heap up empty words as some heathen do, for they think they will be heard for their hundred hollow words. Rather, know that your Father knows what you need even before you ask it. So when you pray, pray this way:

" 'Our Father in heaven,
May your name always be kept holy.
May your kingdom come, your will be done,
On earth as it is in heaven.
Give us today our daily bread,
And forgive us our sins
As we have forgiven those who sinned against us.
Lead us not into temptation,
But deliver us from the evil one.
Amen.'

"Ask, and it will surely be given you," Jesus promised them. "Seek, and you will find. Knock, and the door will be opened unto you. For askers, receive. Seekers do find. And to those who knock, it is opened. Or which of you, when your son asks for bread, gives him a stone instead? Or if your daughter asks for fish, who gives her a snake? Now, if you who are evil give good gifts to your children, how much more will your heavenly Father give good things to those who ask him!"

Jesus looked at the disciples sitting around him. They were rapt and peaceful now, but he saw the troubles and sorrows of their tomorrows. He wanted them, for their own sakes, to put their trust in him.

"Listen," he said, "do not worry about your lives, nervously wondering, 'What will I eat? What will I drink? What will I wear in the morning?' Look at the birds of the air! They sow no seeds, reap no harvest, store no goods in barns—yet your heavenly Father feeds them. Are you not more valuable than they?

"Why do you worry about your clothes? Look at the lilies, which neither spin thread nor weave cloth nor sew it together to wear. Yet even resplendent King Solomon was never dressed like one of these. If God so clothes the grass, which tomorrow is burned away, will he not clothe you even more, you of little faith? Do not worry. Your Father knows you need these things. Seek first his kingdom and his righteousness, and all these things will be given to you as well."

Power Over Sea and Spirits

Then Jesus, his voice husky with weariness, whispered to his closest disciples, "We need to go. Come quickly. We will cross the sea to the other side."

So the boat was shoved from the shore, and Jesus' disciples pulled for the wide water of the sea. Jesus sat in the stern and immediately fell asleep.

He slept deeply. He did not count the hours that passed nor see the stars wink out. He did not feel the sea breeze change into a hard, commanding wind. He did not feel the waves that bunched at the hull of the boat. He did not feel the storm build and begin to rage. The disciples, rowing furiously, began to panic. Still the Master slept.

The waves swelled to tremendous heights, and the wind ripped spray from the tops of them. The boat was swept down into watery valleys, only to swim up again at a violent angle. The disciples were terrified, but still Jesus slept.

"Lord!" they finally shrieked in terror. "Lord!" and they shook him awake. "Don't you care if we drown? Don't you care if we die?"

There was no hurry in his waking up, nor did he hurry to stand in the boat, nor did he lose his balance standing.

Jesus stretched forth his arms and cried to the winds, "Be silent!" and to the waves, "Be still!"

At once the hard wind ceased, and great calm was everywhere. The boat sailed lightly on a peaceful water.

But Jesus did not at once sit down. Even in the darkness the disciples felt his eyes upon them. "Why should you be afraid?" It was the same voice as the one that had commanded the weather. "Do you still have no faith?" Jesus asked.

And when he sat back down, they whispered, "What kind of man is this that even the wind and the waves obey him?"

Early the following morning, several sleepy herdsmen stood near two thousand pigs and watched while thirteen strangers beached a boat. Suddenly a piercing scream cut through the morning. Out of the tombs leaped a man absolutely naked. There were scars on his chest where he had beaten himself, scars on his wrists and his ankles where the herdsmen and others had bound him with ropes and chains. But he had always broken free of their restraints, for his strength was demonic. He was filled with evil spirits.

"What do you want?" screamed the man. "What do you want from me, Jesus, Son of the Most High God?"

Jesus replied, "Spirit, come out of the man!"

"Don't! Don't do this thing!" screamed the man. "Do not torment me!"

"What is your name?" Jesus asked.

"My name," cried the man, shrinking away, "is Legion, for we are not one spirit. We are many. Please, do not send us out of the area," he wept. "There are pigs over there—send us to the pigs," begged the man. "Let us enter the pigs."

"So be it," answered Jesus.

Then the whole herd of pigs, like a carpet come alive, began to sway and to squeal. And just as the herdsmen jumped free, all two thousand pigs turned and charged down the steep embankment, thumping and rolling until they landed every one of them in the sea, where they drowned.

The herdsmen ran into the city and gathered together a great crowd of citizens. Then they all returned to the ridge with a single purpose in mind.

"Go away!" they ordered Jesus. "Leave our country. Leave us alone," they begged the man of mysterious powers.

Jesus offered them no argument. "Let me come with you!" cried the one he had healed.

But Jesus had a better idea. "No. Go home to your friends and tell them how much the Lord has done for you. Tell them what mercy he has had upon you."

When the boat pulled out to sea, the herdsmen became conscious of a vast emptiness in their day.

"The Lord?" they asked one another. "Did he say 'the Lord'?"

Jesus Teaches in Stories

Once when Jesus was teaching from Simon's boat and the crowd sat on shore—the land, the sea, and all the sky being his classroom and everything in them a lesson—the Master stopped short and sat quietly for a while. The boat rocked, and the people wondered at his pausing.

Then he began to teach again, but it did not feel as though he were teaching. Instead, he simply told a story. In some ways, the people felt like little children. They were glad to hear the story, but they were not quite sure why he told it or what it meant.

"Once upon a time," Jesus began, "a farmer went out to sow his seed. He scattered the seed everywhere over the field, so some of it fell on the path, where the birds came and ate it.

"He scattered the seed everywhere, so some of it fell on the rocky ground, where the soil lies thin and warm. Here it

MARK 5; MATTHEW 13

sprouted speedily. But the hot sun scorched the tender plants, and, because they had no roots, they withered.

"He scattered the seed everywhere, so some of it fell among weeds. The weeds and the wheat grew together until the wild weeds choked the good wheat, and it perished.

"But he scattered the seed everywhere over the field, so some seed fell on the good, rich soil. There it grew and produced a crop multiplying thirty, sixty, even a hundred times."

The Teacher sat down, then glanced around at the people. The boat rocked, the people blinked and then stared right back at him. Was that the end of the story?

Yes, that was the end, for now Jesus stood up in the boat and cried out, "Let anyone with ears to hear, listen!" Then he signaled Simon to row him back to shore.

People asked each other what he had been talking about, but no one could explain.

Even the disciples, when they were alone with him, asked, "What were you talking about? Why did you tell us that story?"

"That was more than a story," said Jesus. "That was a parable. You may look at it to enjoy it, but you should look through it to know its meaning, its truth. I give you windows that you might see into the kingdom of God. The farmer, his seed, and the soils—all together they form a window."

"What are we supposed to see through that window?" asked the disciples. "What does the parable mean?"

Then Jesus showed them the meaning. "The seed is like the word of the kingdom," he explained. "When people hear the word but do not understand it, they are like the hard dirt of the path. The evil one snatches away what was sown in their hearts. Some people, like rocky ground, receive the word with joy, but it takes no real root in them. So when persecution rises up like the hot sun, when they are scorned because of the word, they fall away, and the word quickly withers in them.

"The weeds are the worries of this world and the love of its riches. They soon choke the word in some hearts so that it bears no fruit.

"But the good rich soil is the person who hears, understands, and embraces the word. That person indeed bears fruit—thirty, sixty, one hundred times what was sown!

"Do you see?" asked Jesus.

"Now we see," answered the disciples.

"Then keep seeing," Jesus said. "Everywhere there are windows into the kingdom of heaven. Everywhere there are parables!

"Consider the grain of mustard seed. It is the smallest of all seeds, but when it is grown it becomes a tree so great that the birds of the air can make their nests in its branches. The mustard seed is like the kingdom of God, which is beginning so small but will grow into something great.

"Or you—Simon, John—look at the net you used to fish with. You threw it into the sea and gathered fish of every kind. When it was full, you pulled it ashore, sat down, and sorted the bad from the good. The good you kept; the bad you tossed away. Now, the kingdom of heaven is like the net! For so it will be when this age is over. The angels will sort the evil from the righteous and toss those who are evil into the fiery furnace.

"Do you see?" Jesus asked them again. "Do you understand?"

"Yes!" said the disciples. "Stories that are more than stories! We do see!"

"Then blessed are your eyes," said Jesus, "for they see what the prophets yearned to see but did not. Blessed are your ears, for they hear the voice of God."

Two Lessons on Faith

Thus Jesus ministered throughout Galilee, preaching the word of the kingdom, healing the hurt, liberating people oppressed by the devil. How great was the heart of the Master for the crowds! How deep and abiding his love for them!

"Jeeeee-sus!" the people cried in delight as Jesus stepped out of the boat. They sang his name again and again, until he had climbed a small hill and sat down. Then they gathered around him as closely as they could and listened to his every word.

The disciples sat by their boat through the long afternoon. They thought of a cool drink in the shade, for the sun was hot. They thought of different kinds of food, for the evening was near and no one had eaten.

Finally Philip and Andrew went to Jesus and whispered in his ear, "Lord, send the people away. This is a remote place. For their own sakes, send them back to the villages where they can buy something to eat."

But Jesus spoke aloud. "Philip, how do you propose we should feed them?"

The people heard that. Philip was embarrassed. "We?" he

whispered. "Lord, we can't do that! Wages for two hundred days' work is not enough to buy that much bread!"

"How much bread do we have with us?" Jesus asked loudly.

Andrew whispered, "There is a boy here with five barley loaves and two small fish. I'm afraid that's all the food we have."

"But I am here," said Jesus, "and I know precisely what I am going to do! Tell the people to sit down."

Obediently, Philip carried this word to the other disciples, and soon thousands were seated in groups of fifties and hundreds.

When everyone was seated, Jesus took the bread, looked up to heaven, and gave thanks. Then he broke the loaf and gave it to his disciples to distribute. He divided the fish in the same way. The food went out to everyone, and everyone ate, and everyone was filled. More than five thousand were satisfied when the hand of the Lord touched five loaves of bread and two small fish.

"Philip!" Jesus called. Then he whispered in that disciple's ear, "Gather up the fragments, that nothing be lost."

When the people saw the baskets full of crumbs, the miracle of their meal struck them. Each disciple took a basket to the boat. Twelve disciples, twelve baskets! Twelve baskets full of what they could not eat!

Immediately Jesus sent the disciples to the boat, telling them to go on without him while he dismissed the crowd.

They were six hours at sea, lapped in utter darkness. The noise of the crowd had faded into the distance, but the noise of the wind and the waves had arisen. That was a lonely, frightening howl.

Suddenly, in a terrified voice, James whispered, "Look!"

They all looked. Rowing stopped. The boat swung loose and rolled.

A dim, wispy figure seemed to be floating on the water not too far from them.

"What is it?"

"I don't know. I don't know."

"Look! It's coming closer!"

"A ghost!" cried James. "It's a ghost!"

The boat tossed. The disciples gripped the sides and cried out in terror. Then the figure spoke to them.

"Do not be afraid," said a familiar voice. Then Jesus himself, walking toward them on the water, called, "It is I."

Immediately Peter stood up in the boat and laughed. "Lord, if it's really you, let me come to you on the water!"

Jesus said, "Come."

Simon stepped over the side and onto the water, big and bold and walking!

But then—halfway between the boat and the Lord—Peter suddenly realized what he was doing. He stopped. He put out his arms for balance. And very cautiously he spoke one reasonable word: "Maybe..."

In that instant he sank into the sea.

"Lord!" he spluttered. "Save me!" he coughed.

Jesus reached down and caught him. "Oh, Simon of so little faith!" he said as he carried the fisherman back to his boat.

Then the winds ceased, and Simon did little rowing after that.

The disciples worshiped Jesus, saying, "Truly, you are the Son of God."

Religious Opposition Grows

"We've been watching you!"

This angry declaration was flung at Jesus by certain Pharisees, who were determined to strictly obey all of the laws.

"You break the Sabbath laws," they announced. "You permit your disciples to pick grain to eat on the Sabbath. Picking grain is work, and work is prohibited by Sabbath laws. You yourself, as we have noted, heal on the Sabbath—again, work and the breaking of laws. Your disciples persist in ignoring the traditions of the elders. They eat with their hands unwashed. Now, tell us, Teacher: How can you righteously allow such loose, unrighteous living?"

"You," said Jesus, his eyes flashing, "you hypocrites! You ignore God's commands to chase after human traditions! You give a tenth of your insignificant spices—mint, dill, and cumin—but you neglect the weightier matters of the law: justice, mercy, and faith! You blind guides! You strain an unclean gnat out of your water but swallow an unclean camel!"

"Well!" said the Pharisees around him. Jesus fought hard and suddenly. But they would return the fight with a test.

"Well, Teacher," they said, "if you are free to ignore the laws of our ancestors, prove it. Give us some sign from heaven that we may know you have the right to do what you do."

Jesus sighed deeply at their mocking request; their hard,

unseeing hearts both saddened and angered him.

"An evil and adulterous generation asks for a sign," he said. "But there will be no sign except for the sign of the prophet Jonah. For just as Jonah was three days and three nights in the belly of the fish, so will I, the Son of Man, be three days and three nights in the heart of the earth. Pay attention! Someone greater than Jonah is here!"

"Some way," thought the religious leaders as they left, "some way we will mute that man!"

But now Jesus led his disciples away from them and the crowds for a while, away from Capernaum, away from Galilee, off into northern regions where they could be alone.

The Truth About Jesus

In a small garden apart from anyone else, Jesus sat with his disciples, his back to the grizzled roots of an olive tree. Almost casually he asked, "What do you hear? Who do the people say the Son of Man is?"

The disciples smiled at the things they had heard.

"Some say you are John the Baptizer come back from the dead."

"Elijah. I have heard you called Elijah."

"Or Jeremiah."

"They think you are one of the prophets come back again."

Jesus leaned forward and fixed his eyes upon them. "But who do you say I am?"

Simon answered immediately, almost shouting the words.

"You are the Christ," he exclaimed, "the Son of the living God!"

Quiet followed that confession. Then Jesus arose, walked to Simon, and took him by his shoulders. "Blessed are you, Simon!" he said, gazing into the big man's eyes. "This was revealed to you, not by any person, but by my Father, who is in heaven. You are Peter, the rock. On this rock I will build my church, and the powers of death shall not be able to stand against it."

Suddenly he turned toward all of the disciples. "I must leave soon," he said. "Understand what I am about to say to you. I must soon go to Jerusalem, and what will take place there will seem no victory. I must go to suffer many things at the hands of the authorities in Jerusalem..."

"No!" interrupted Simon Peter.

"So it must be," said Jesus without hesitation, keeping his back to that disciple. "In that place, I will be killed..."

"No!" shouted Simon, standing up.

"So it must be!" Jesus repeated. "Then, on the third day, I will be raised from the dead..."

"God forbid it!" roared Simon Peter, as he grabbed Jesus. "Lord, this shall never happen to you!" He tried to turn the Teacher to look him squarely in the eyes.

But Jesus stood as hard as a stone and would not turn. His back to Simon Peter, he uttered stinging words: "Get out of my sight, Satan!" The thick man stumbled backward and sat with a thud, like a bundle of straw. "Your cares are human cares. Your thoughts do not come from God," said Jesus, "and you are holding me back!"

Silence had followed Peter's confession; silence now followed his folly. Jesus walked back to the olive tree while every disciple concentrated on holding very still.

"Disciples," said Jesus, facing the tree. "Is that what you really are? If any want to be my disciples, let them deny themselves, let them take up their cross, and let them follow me. For those who seek to save their lives will lose them instead. But those who lose their lives for my sake will find them. Oh, my little children! What will you have if you should gain the whole world but lose your life in the process?"

Simon Peter was a subdued and sorry figure after that. It felt as though he did everything wrong, so he determined to do nothing at all. Great Peter became great gloom among the disciples, and for five days he sat alone, brooding.

Then, on the sixth day, Jesus touched him on the shoulder and said, "Come with us."

Peter looked around. James and John were standing close by. "Where?" he asked.

"Come with us," Jesus repeated and walked away. Jesus led the three up the side of a mountain, a high mountain with a grassy meadow at the top. There Jesus raised his arms toward heaven and began in a low voice to pray.

Peter thought that perhaps he too should pray, so he began to raise his own arms—then suddenly the face of the Lord began to change. It grew brighter and brighter until it shone like the sun. Even his clothes glistened! The brilliance so flooded Peter's head that he squinted and felt dizzy at the sight.

Then, look! Two men standing with Jesus! It was Moses and Elijah! They were talking with Jesus, discussing his journey to Jerusalem!

Peter didn't know whether to laugh or to cry, so full was he with the excitement of the moment. But when he saw that Moses and Elijah were leaving, he cried out, "Master! It is good for us to be here! Let us make three shrines—one for you, one for Moses, one for Elijah!"

Then a rolling, mighty cloud came down upon them, and the words died on his lips for the fear that he felt. Suddenly a voice thundered from the cloud, saying, "This is my Son, whom I love. Listen to him!"

Peter collapsed and lay trembling with awe. Both James and John fell down on either side of him, and they might have lain there for days—but Jesus came and touched them.

"Rise," he said in a familiar voice, "and don't be afraid."

Peter lifted up his eyes, looked around, and saw no one but Jesus. And with what new eyes he looked upon his Lord! His dark gloom was gone, and ever afterward he remembered this bright event with joy.

Lessons on Forgiveness

Once Jesus was standing in a public place, speaking to the crowd, when a band of self-righteous Pharisees—their eyebrows pinched, their lips drawn tight, their chins raised high—marched through the crowd and into Jesus' presence.

They shoved a woman before Jesus and commanded her,

"Stand there!" She did, her face buried in her hands.

"Master!" they announced. "This woman was caught in the act of adultery. In the very act, mind you! Now, we are well aware of the law, that Moses commands us to stone such a sinner. But we thought that we would ask you. What do you say we should do to her?"

For all their solemnity, this was no serious question—except that they meant to trap him in his words. Would he say to stone her to death? Why, then he would be violating Roman law and his own teachings on compassion and forgiveness. Would he say to let her live? Then he would be a lawbreaker. Condemn him!

Jesus said nothing.

He glanced at the poor, frightened woman, then squatted and began to write in the dust with his finger.

Several minutes passed in silence. Finally Jesus looked up and said, "Let the man among you who is without sin cast the first stone." Then he returned to writing.

One by one, the woman's accusers slinked away.

Several more minutes passed silently. Finally Jesus stood up and looked around. "Woman, where are your accusers?" he asked. "Did no one condemn you?"

"No one, Lord," she said.

"Then neither do I condemn you." Jesus declared. "Go now, and sin no more."

And what was the light that shone on her face and that shone in her face thereafter? Why, it was Jesus himself. For he said before all of the people, "I AM the light of the world!

Anyone who follows me will not walk in darkness but will have the light of life!"

Once, to help people understand how God felt about sinners, Jesus told a parable. "Once upon a time," he began, "there was a father who had two sons. One day the younger son said, 'Father, I can't wait. Give me my share of the inheritance now.' So the father divided his goods and gave to the younger all that he asked for.

"Soon the younger son converted the goods into money, left home with a fat purse, and traveled to a far country.

"Now, this part of the story will not surprise you. There he lived recklessly, spending his money without a thought or a care until the last penny had vanished. Unfortunately, when a famine struck the land, the young man poor became a young man hungry. The only job he found was to feed another man's pigs. He grew so hungry that he would have gladly eaten the pods that the pigs ate—but no one gave him anything.

"Finally he came to his senses and said, 'Back home, my father's servants have bread enough and some to spare, but here I'm dying of hunger! I know what I'll do. I'll go back to my father and confess that I've sinned against heaven and against him. 'I'm not worthy to be your son,' I will say. 'Treat me simply as a servant.'

"So the young man left the pigpen, his head hanging low, his body and his soul together very weak, and walked home.

"Even while he was some distance away, his father saw him. The man was so filled with compassion for his son that he ran to meet him, hugged him, and kissed him.

"But the son put up his hands, saying, 'Father, no! I have sinned against heaven and before you. I am not worthy...'

" 'Don't say another word!' replied his father. Then he called to the servants, 'Bring the best robe and put it on my son! Put a ring on his finger and shoes on his feet. Butcher a calf for a feast. For this my son was dead, and now he is alive. My son was lost, and he is found!'

"While everyone else was celebrating in the house, the elder son came home from the fields. He heard the music, but he did not understand it, since no one had told him about a party.

" 'What's going on in there?' he asked a servant. Then, as the servant told him, his face soured and his jaw clenched. 'You tell my father,' he said bitterly, 'that I will have nothing to do with a party for that sinful son of his!'

"When the father came outside to urge his elder son to join the celebration, the son refused, 'No! All these years I have worked for you, never disobeying you. Yet you never gave me a party. But the moment this squanderer comes home, you kill a calf and throw a party. No. I will not join his party.'

" 'My son, you are always with me,' said the father, 'and all that I have is always yours. But your brother was dead! He was lost. Surely it is right to rejoice at his restoration!' "

The Final Journey Begins

There came a morning, finally, when the disciples found Jesus already awake and on the road before them. But he was not walking. He stood silently looking south, gazing with great, dark eyes in the direction of Jerusalem. Galilee was behind him.

"It is nearly time," he said, when all twelve disciples had gathered. "We are going to Jerusalem."

Then he began immediately to walk; the disciples followed, amazed and afraid.

"He is a good man."

"No! He is leading the people astray!"

But those who believed in him asked, "Could anyone possibly perform more signs than this man has?"

"Signs? Why, this man has an evil spirit and works his magic by the power of the devil!"

"No," some replied. "Jesus is the Christ, the Messiah."

"How can you say that? The Scriptures say that the Messiah is to come from the line of David and from the town of Bethlehem. But this man—he comes from Galilee!"

So went the talk all up and down the land. There was a division among the people. Some loved him completely, believed in him, and devoted themselves to him. Some hated him, feared him, and sought some grounds for which they might arrest him.

And as Jesus traveled slowly to Jerusalem, the feelings intensified: Love grew the warmer and hate the hotter...

Thus Jesus moved slowly and methodically toward Jerusalem, teaching, preaching, and healing on the way. Thus the word went out from every place where he paused, the word of his marvelous deeds: how between Galilee and Samaria he healed ten lepers, only one of whom—and a Samaritan, at that—returned to thank him; how he gave sight to blind Bartimaeus outside Jericho; how he called Zacchaeus, a tax collector in Jericho, down from a sycamore tree and moved him to repay all he had stolen.

The word went out. People heard that word. Again the crowds swelled around Jesus wherever he went. People were alive with excitement because it seemed that something great was soon to happen, something they should witness.

Jesus spoke to them about that something, but he did so in the gentlest terms.

"I AM the good shepherd," he said. "The good shepherd lays down his life for the sheep.

"My sheep hear my voice and follow me, and I give them eternal life. They shall never perish! No one shall snatch them out of my hand! My Father, who has given them to me, is greater than all; no one can snatch them from the Father's hand. I and the Father are one."

So spoke the Lord, and a few began to understand that all his miracles were merely signs to point their hearts to him. These believed in him. But others followed him because they liked to be fed or because they were looking for someone to lead them in revolt against the oppressive Romans. Still others hated him and were drawn perversely to the object of their hatred. The crowd was a tense, restless body in those final days.

Jesus Raises the Dead

His last pause and his last visitation, his last miracle before Jerusalem happened in this way.

Jesus was staying east of the Jordan River when a messenger, haggard from a hard run, found Jesus and told him that his friend Lazarus was deathly ill. Jesus thanked him for the information, sent him on his way, and promptly went back to what he had been doing. For two more days he did nothing about the illness. Only when Jesus knew in his heart that Lazarus had died did he mention to his disciples that they must now go to Bethany, to Lazarus.

This idleness was remarkable, for Lazarus was the brother of Mary and Martha, and all three were loved by the Lord. Why should he wait until the man was dead before he went to him? "That God's glory might shine in God's Son," Jesus answered. But who could understand such words?

"Why go to Bethany now?" the disciples asked. "It's too close to Jerusalem. You know people there are planning to kill you."

"Because our brother Lazarus has fallen asleep, and I must go waken him," said Jesus.

"Asleep? Is that all?" The disciples did not understand these words either. "Let the man sleep! It's good for someone in his condition."

Then Jesus told them plainly. "Lazarus is dead. We must go for his sake—and for yours as well, that you may believe in me." Then he turned and began walking toward Bethany.

Thomas, looking at Jesus' back, said to the other disciples. "We should also go. It is right for us to die with our Lord." So they followed him.

"Lord!" cried Martha, running down the road to meet him. "Lord!" She ran with the loose gait of someone altogether broken by grief. Jesus could see that she had been crying. "Four days ago," she wailed. She fell on his shoulders. He held her up, and his heart ached for her.

Then her words were muffled at his breast. "Why didn't you come earlier? If you had been here, my brother wouldn't have died, wouldn't have died four days ago. But even now God will give you whatever you ask..."

"Martha," said Jesus, his chin brushing her head, "your brother will rise again."

"I know that," she said, but she continued to cry. "He will rise on the last day. But what good is that on *this* day?"

Now Jesus held her away from him and gazed into her eyes. "Martha, listen to me," he said. "Martha, I AM the resurrection and the life! Those who believe in me, even though they die, will live, and everyone who lives and believes in me shall never die! Do you believe this?"

Martha's tears had ceased. She returned Jesus' gaze with a suddenly quiet wonder. "Yes, Lord," she whispered. "I believe that you are the Christ, the Son of God."

Then Jesus asked, "Please bring Mary to me."

When Mary saw Jesus, she fell at his feet and sobbed, "If only you had been here..."

Jesus closed his eyes and touched his temple, for Mary's tears made him very sad. "Where have you laid him?" he asked. Then he also began to cry softly.

"Look how he loved the man!" the people whispered.

They all followed a rising path that ended at a cliff. "Lord, that one." Martha pointed at a tomb closed by a rock.

Jesus said, "Remove the rock from its entrance."

"Oh, Lord, the body is four days in the tomb," said Martha. "Already there is a stench."

"I told you," replied Jesus, "that if you believe, you will see the glory of God. Remove the rock."

When the tomb yawned dark and open, Jesus raised his eyes to heaven and said aloud, "Father, I thank you that you have heard me!" Then, more quietly, "Always you do hear me, but I say this for the people, that they may believe you sent me."

Then Jesus gazed deep into the tomb and cried in a loud voice, "Lazarus! Come out!"

With not so much as a sigh, the dead man appeared in the entrance, his hands and feet wrapped in strips of linen, his face covered with a cloth.

"Take off the grave clothes," said Jesus, "and let him go."

Jesus Sentenced to Death

Many people believed in Jesus for what he did and cried their acclaim of him, but others rushed immediately with bitter report to the religious leaders who hated Jesus.

So the chief leaders called the council together to discuss this dangerous Jesus.

"He works wonders," they said. "He's rousing the people so that they mass around him."

"The Romans will not look kindly on such activity. When they see mobs, they see rebellion!"

"So they slaughter the mobs."

"The mobs, to be sure—but not the mobs only. They crush the people and destroy every sign of strength."

"Including the Temple! Including our whole nation!"

"And where will that leave us?"

"Powerless! We will be puppets. We will be nothing."

"So what are we going to do? In God's name, what will we do about this Jesus?"

Then Caiaphas, the high priest, rose and spoke. "Don't you understand?" he said. "It is better that one man should die for the people than that the whole nation should perish." From that day forward they made serious plans to put Jesus to death.

Now all the things of Jesus' life became one thing, and all the roads he traveled, one road. It is in this thing that the loving Father gave his one and only Son to all people, that everyone who believes in him should not perish but have eternal life.

Sunday: Triumphal Entry

Thus it came to pass that Jesus stood outside the village of Bethphage, gazing at Jerusalem in the distance. It was time to enter that city, death being now but five days away...

"Go into the village," he said to two disciples. "You will find a donkey that has never been ridden. Untie it and bring it to me. If anyone questions you, simply say, 'The Lord has need of it.' "

The crowd forever at his back—the seekers, the believers, the zealots, and the watchers—they saw the disciples go. They searched the face of Jesus for some indication of what was going on but saw only that he was gazing at Jerusalem.

When the disciples returned with the donkey, however, the crowd began to buzz. "Jerusalem!" they cried. "He is going to Jerusalem!"

Then, when the disciples threw their garments over the back of the beast, the buzzing swelled into a low roar. Groups of runners broke from the crowd and dashed toward the city, crying, "He is coming! The Christ is coming!"

And when Jesus himself mounted the donkey and began to ride toward Jerusalem, a thousand throats opened up in jubilation and in song: "Praise to the Son of David! Praise!"

People tossed their garments down in front of Jesus, pleased to have his donkey walk on them. People cut branches and spread them in his path. People raised their hands high in victory, running beside him, running behind him. And in a mighty thunder roll they roared, "Blessed is the King who comes in the name of the Lord! Praise to God in heaven!"

Down from the Mount of Olives, he rode on and into Jerusalem, where another crowd was surging forth to meet him. Even the children were shouting, "Praise to the Son of David!"

The chief priests knifed their way through the crowd, utterly confounded by this procession and terrified by what the Romans would make of it. They snatched at Jesus' clothing and shouted, "Silence them! Silence them! They are calling you all the names of the Messiah! Silence them!"

But Jesus answered, "If these were silent, the stones themselves would cry out loud."

The lines were drawn. It was only a matter of time.

Mark 11; Luke 19

Monday: Temple Cleansing

The next day, Jesus arrived at the Temple with a heavy heart. The outer court, the Court of the Gentiles, looked like a marketplace. Here the meat was alive, still mooing, cooing, bellowing, bleating, caged, tethered, and roped. Here the animals of sacrifice were for sale. Here money was changed from Roman coin to Temple currency. Here tables were set up and business was transacted. The priests were conducting God's business for their own profit.

Into the Court of the Gentiles, like a devouring fire that would not be quenched or turned aside, stormed Jesus.

He stood in the open and cried, "My Father's house! My Father's house!" with such sharp accusation that the buyers and sellers fell silent and stared at him nervously.

"It is written in the prophet Isaiah," said Jesus, pacing among them, " 'My house shall be called a house of prayer for all nations.' But you!" he cried, suddenly overturning a table that had been holding money. The coins spun a thousand different ways. "You!" he shouted, breaking cages and setting free the birds inside, tossing tables, driving back the people. "You have turned it into a den of robbers!"

Then, taking a whip in hand, he drove the merchants, their sheep, and their cattle out of the Temple court.

The chief priests stood by, trembling in their anger. They did nothing then, for they feared the people who still followed Jesus and listened to him. But in their minds they thought furiously of how they would silence him.

Tuesday: Teaching and Treachery

Toward the Mount of Olives Jesus led his disciples. As they walked, the disciples discussed the Temple building—what an excellent piece of work it was, how beautiful were its stones, how admirably and solidly they were joined together!

But Jesus shook his head in warning. "The time is coming," he said, "when it will be destroyed so completely that not one stone will be left standing on another."

This thought itched in the minds of the disciples, so later, when they were sitting on the Mount of Olives, they asked, "When, Lord? When will the Temple be demolished? Also, what will be the signs of your return and of the end of this age?"

Slowly, carefully, Jesus answered. "Be careful that no one deceives you," he warned, "for many will come in my name, saying, 'I am the Christ.' Do not believe them. You will hear of wars and rumors of wars; even then do not be alarmed. The end is not yet. Nation will rise up against nation, and there will be famines and earthquakes. These are not signs of the end—they are just the beginning of the birth pains.

"Then people will persecute you and put you to death. You will be despised by all the nations for the sake of my name. Then many will fall away from me, betraying and hating one another. In the spreading wickedness, love will grow cold. But the one who endures to the end shall be saved!

"When the good news of the kingdom of God has been preached throughout the entire world, then the end will come. It will not come with the destruction of the Temple. It will come with the spread of the gospel. This is the sign of the end.

"The end. The sun will be darkened, the moon wink out, the stars fall down from the sky, and the powers of the heavens will be shaken. Then all the peoples of the world will see the Son of Man coming on the clouds of heaven. He will send out his angels with the blast of a trumpet, and they will gather his chosen people from the four winds, from one end of heaven to the other. Then, only then, is it the end.

"But listen to me," Jesus said with an intensity that none of them forgot. "No one can tell you when the end will come. Of that day and that hour, no one knows—not the angels in heaven, not even the Son. The Father alone, he knows. Therefore, watch! Be ready! Always, always be ready.

"For when the day of judgment arrives, when the Son of Man descends in all his glory," continued Jesus, "he will sit on his throne. Before him shall stand the nations of the world. Then he shall separate people as a shepherd separates sheep from goats, the sheep on the right, the goats to the left.

"To those upon his right hand, the King will say, 'Come, O blessed of my Father! Come, inherit the kingdom prepared for you from the beginning of time. For I was hungry and you gave me food; I was thirsty and you gave me drink; I was a stranger and you welcomed me, naked and you clothed me, sick and you cared for me, in prison and you visited me.'

"But the righteous will ask, 'Lord, when did we see you hungry and feed you, or thirsty and give you drink? When did we welcome you as a stranger, clothe you, or visit you?'

"Then the King will answer them, 'When you did it to

one of the least of these my people, you did it to me.'

"Next he will say to those on his left, 'Away from me, you cursed! Away to the fires eternal, burning for the devil and all of his angels! For I was hungry, but you gave me no food; thirsty, but you gave me no drink. I was a stranger who found no welcome from you, naked and given no clothing by you, sick and no care, imprisoned and no visit!'

" 'When, Lord?' the wicked will ask, shocked at the sentence and gravely ignorant of their crime. 'When did we see you in need and do none of these things for you?'

" 'In truth, when you denied kindness to the least of these,' the King will explain, 'you denied kindness to me.'

"Then the wicked will go away to eternal punishment, but the righteous to life everlasting."

When Jesus finished teaching, he rose and returned to Bethany. He had need of a rest. Friday was not far off.

Because Judas Iscariot carried the money for the disciples, it was not unusual for him to go off alone to purchase bread or some other necessity.

Therefore, when he left Jesus and the others, frowning so thoughtfully that his black eyebrows nearly covered his eyes, no one asked, "Where are you going?" Everyone supposed that he knew where Judas Iscariot was headed.

"Does anyone know the habits of Jesus? Does anyone know him that well?"

When Judas had heard the chief priests asking those questions, he had thought, "Who knows Jesus better than I?"

Little did the disciples know that Judas was going to the Temple, to the chief priests, to sell Jesus and not to buy bread.

Judas was shrewd in business, cunning at the trading table, convinced that he could accomplish his own will in every exchange. Why else would he hold the one purse for the Twelve? Now his eyebrows narrowed, and he began to bargain.

"How much will you give me," he asked the chief priests, "if I deliver unto you Jesus of Nazareth?"

The chief priests raised their eyebrows in interest.

"Do you know Jesus?" they asked.

"Very well," he said.

"Do you know his habits?"

"As well as any man."

"Do you know some private place to which he retires, some place where the crowds do not follow him?"

"Yes," said Judas. His eyes relaxed. He knew such a place.

"Understand that we cannot arrest him openly," said the chief priests. "The people would riot and the whole purpose of this important labor would be lost. Time and place are critical; make them late and lonely, if you can."

Judas, shrewd bargainer, giving so little to get so much, merely replied, "I can do that."

"Then you are a friend to us, Judas Iscariot," smiled the chief priests, "and we take care of our friends." Carefully, they weighed thirty pieces of silver into his hand, which hand dropped them not into the common purse but into his own. Then Judas left, content. A lot of money for so little information! It had been a successful conversation.

Thursday: The Final Hours

The time for the Passover feast was at hand, so Jesus sent Peter and John to prepare the meal for him and the Twelve. He told them exactly where to find the right person who would allow them to use the right place to celebrate the feast. Ever obedient, Peter and John did everything exactly as Jesus had instructed.

There was an uncomfortable moment at the beginning of the meal. Everyone was at table, yet no one spoke and no one ate. In profound silence, with eyes filled with love and sadness, Jesus gazed one by one at each of the disciples.

He knew that it was time for him to leave his disciples, to return to his Father. He knew also who would betray him.

Judas rolled a wine cup between his hands, frowning.

Simon Peter looked directly back at Jesus and smiled nervously. Jesus didn't return his smile.

John, reclining next to Jesus, looked quizzically and then expectantly at the Master.

James and Philip and Thomas, Matthew, Bartholomew, Andrew, and James of Alphaeus, the other Simon, and the other Judas all reclined around the table in various attitudes of expectation or uncertainty. "What is coming? What is he thinking?" Their legs and feet extended from the low table; they leaned on their elbows.

Suddenly Jesus arose, laid his robe aside, and wrapped a towel around his waist. Then he poured water into a pitcher, bent down, and washed the feet of the nearest disciple, John.

LUKE 22; JOHN 13

After drying John's feet with the towel, Jesus went to the next disciple and did the same. One by one, Jesus washed his disciples' feet...until he came to Peter.

Peter drew back his feet and sat on them. "Lord, are you going to wash my feet?" he asked.

Jesus, kneeling before Peter, answered, "You do not now understand what I am doing, but you will understand in the future."

"No!" said Peter, shaking his head. "No, Lord. You will never wash my feet!"

Jesus began to stand up, "Peter, if I do not wash you, you have no part with me."

Immediately Peter changed his mind. He stuck out not only his feet but hands, arms, shoulders, head. "Then, Lord, my feet and my hands and my head..."

"Ah, Simon my rock," Jesus interrupted, "the one who has bathed has no need to wash, except for the feet. That one is clean all over. And you, my disciples, you *are* clean, except for one of you."

Judas rolled his wine cup between his palms, staring at the red inside.

When Jesus finished washing the feet of all twelve disciples, he robed and reclined again. Then he said, "Do you understand what I have done for you? You call me 'Lord,' and rightly so. You call me 'Master,' and so you should, for so I am. Now if I, your Lord and your Master, wash your feet, certainly you should do the same for one another. Learn from me, remember my example," said the Lord, "and serve each other in love."

The roasted lamb went around the table, the disciples cutting portions for themselves, the disciples eating. Bread also was handed from one to another, the disciples breaking pieces for themselves, dipping it in sauce, and eating. But amidst the happy feasting, an inexpressible grief pulled at the corners of the Lord's lips. He breathed deeply and sighed.

"Truly," he said softly, "truly, I say to you—one of you will betray me."

At once the eating stopped.

The disciples stared at one another. They began to chatter excitedly, nervously, "Lord, is it I? Is it I?"

Without moving, without raising his voice, as though he had not heard their questions, Jesus replied, "The Son of Man shall now go step for step as it was determined he would go. But woe to the one by whom he is betrayed! It would be better for that man if he had never been born!"

Peter signaled to John that he should ask Jesus who the betrayer was. Leaning closer to Jesus, John whispered, "Who, Lord? Who is the man?"

Jesus said, "I am going to dip this piece of bread in the dish. The one to whom I hand the bread—he is the man."

Judas did not so much as blink when Jesus handed him the bread. "What you are about to do, do quickly," Jesus said. Then Judas arose and silently passed into the night.

This meal had become like no other meal the disciples had ever eaten. The next thing that Jesus did fixed it in their minds forever.

He took the Passover bread—the bread made without yeast—and pronounced a blessing over it. Then he broke it and gave it to his disciples, saying, "Take it. Eat it. This is my body."

Slowly they chewed the bread and swallowed it, watching Jesus. His body!

Next he took the cup, gave thanks to God, and gave the cup to them with the words: "Drink this, all of you. It is my blood of the new covenant, my blood shed for many people for the forgiveness of sins."

They passed the cup around, each taking a drink from it. His blood!

"I tell you the truth," said Jesus. "I will not again drink of the fruit of the vine until the day I drink it in my Father's kingdom, when I drink it again with you, my friends."

"It is now about to happen," Jesus said into the silence of the room, "and the Son of Man is nearly glorified. Little children, I am leaving you..."

Peter stiffened to hear these words. But he struggled not to talk. He should not talk! "...and though you will seek me, where I am going you cannot come."

You cannot come! The words struck Peter like a rod, but he ground his teeth and fought the impulse to talk. He talked too much. He should not talk!

"So I am giving you a new commandment," continued Jesus, "both for yourselves and for a witness to all the world, that the world may know me through you. Love one another. Even as I love you, love one another. By this will all people know that you are my disciples, if you love one another..."

Peter exploded. "Why, Lord? Why can't I follow you, Lord?" His tone was almost brutal; it came from an aggressive love.

Jesus regarded the strong disciple with gentle understanding and said, "You will, Peter. You will certainly follow the path that I am going to take—but later, not now."

"Why not?" Peter demanded. "Why can't I follow you right now?"

"Oh, Peter, the things you don't understand," said Jesus. "Because, my friend, you are not strong enough." Peter was visibly stung by that. Jesus continued, "This very night each one of you will desert me, scattering like sheep when their shepherd is attacked . . ."

"Not me!" Peter struck his chest. "They might. Andrew might. James and John might desert you, but not me! Lord, I will follow you even to prison, even to death!"

"Peter!" Jesus spoke sharply, then closed his eyes. That gesture always disabled the rash disciple. "Peter," Jesus said with his eyes still closed, "before the rooster crows an end to this night, you will deny me three times!"

Peter was reduced to mumbling. "No, I will not," he mumbled. "They can threaten me with death, and still I will not deny you."

Miserably bewildered, Peter and the other disciples stared at their plates, neither eating nor speaking.

Suddenly Jesus smiled and said, "Don't be upset! You believe in God. Believe also in me. In my Father's house are many, many rooms. I am going to prepare a place for you, and then I will return to take you to myself, that where I am you may also be. You know the way to the place where I'm going."

Thomas fairly shouted, "No, Lord! We do not know where you are going! How can we know the way?"

"The way," said Jesus, gazing warmly at Thomas. "Look at me, Thomas. I AM the way and the truth and the life. No one comes to the Father but through me. If you really knew me, you would know the Father. But from now on you do know him; you have seen him.

"Children, children!" Jesus said with a soft, comforting love. "I am not going to leave you here as orphans. When I am gone, I will send you another from the Father. I will send the Counselor, the Holy Spirit, the Spirit of Truth. He will be my witness, teaching you everything and reminding you of all that I have said to you.

"Peace I leave with you. My peace I give unto you. So do not be troubled. Don't be afraid."

Then Jesus stood up, walked to the door, and opened it. It was dark night outside.

"I will not say much more to you," he said, "because the ruler of this world is coming. Understand that he has no power over me to take my life. I myself do freely lay it down. I lay down my life because I love you, my friends, and because I always obey the will of the Father.

"Come, now. Let's find a private place where there will be no crowds."

So Jesus, his robe closed tight against the night wind, and his eleven disciples walked into the dark night of Jerusalem.

Jesus prayed aloud to the Father as they walked, asking God to keep all who believed in him: to keep them safe, to keep them joyful, to keep them in the truth, to keep them one.

Eventually they crossed the Kidron Valley and came to the Mount of Olives, to a secluded spot called Gethsemane— quiet, private, and apart.

As they entered the Garden of Gethsemane, Jesus murmured, "My soul is heavy with sorrow, even unto death."

These words burned in Simon Peter. But he had no words of comfort for his friend, for his Lord.

"Wait here," said Jesus. "Please stay awake." Then he walked on until darkness enveloped him. "Father!" Jesus wailed, collapsing to the ground, a horrified cry in the night. "Father," he repeated with his cheek against the earth, "Father," he prayed, "if it is possible, remove this cup from me." Sweat broke on his forehead and ran down his face in heavy blood-like drops.

Long, long the Lord lay curled upon the earth, asking God for his life. Then, in the midst of his agony and anguish, Jesus said, "Yet not my will, Father, your will be done."

Softly he returned to the three disciples.

"Peter? John? James?"

There was no answer.

He put his hands to their faces and found them sleeping. "Could you not wait for me even one hour?" he whispered.

He shook Peter's shoulder. "Wake up!" he commanded. "Stay awake and pray that you do not give in to temptation. Peter, your spirit indeed is willing, but your flesh is weak."

Peter, greatly ashamed, groaned and struggled to stand up.

Jesus shook John, saying, "It is time, now. The Son of Man is about to be delivered into the hands of sinners." Likewise, he woke James. "Arise. The betrayer is at hand."

The three disciples were confused and guilty and foggy from their sleeping. They didn't know what to say...

Chink, chink! Chink, chink!

A distant sound, like an alarm, brought them suddenly, soberly awake.

Chink, chink! CHINK, CHINK!

Metal on metal! They stared toward Jerusalem and perceived a line of torches winking through the trees. Soldiers!

Suddenly a detachment of soldiers, led by Judas, stepped out of the darkness and surrounded the small band of men. Just as suddenly, Judas stepped out of the crowd, identified Jesus, and betrayed Jesus with a kiss on the cheek. The soldiers immediately seized Jesus and led him away. The disciples, frightened sheep, scattered in every direction.

The walls were lined with chief priests and others who wanted to see Jesus condemned. Jesus himself stood alone in the center of the room, the folds of his robe falling in perfectly straight lines from his shoulders to the floor.

"Testimony!" This hasty trial was taking place in the house of the high priest. His own people filled the courtyard outside the door; no friends of Jesus waited there...except Simon Peter, who had quietly slipped into the yard and stood warming himself by a fire.

"Testimony!" demanded Caiaphas, the high priest. "Bring me witnesses against this man, and tell me the crime that shall put him to death! Testimony!"

A man peeled himself from the wall and stepped forward. "I heard..."

"Speak up!" Caiaphas commanded.

The man shouted in a ridiculously high voice, "I heard Jesus say he would destroy the Temple, the Temple of God, and build it up again in three days."

"So did I!" another man cried immediately. "So did I! Those were his words, his very words!" Neither man looked at Jesus, for they were testifying falsely.

Caiaphas smiled and leaned forward in his chair. "Well, Jesus of Nazareth," he said. "You have heard the testimony, accusations of a very damning sort. How do you answer them?"

The chief priests wet their lips, for they were ready to counter by studied arguments whatever Jesus said. The scribes folded their arms, for they would hate whatever Jesus said. The servants set their teeth, for they would hiss whatever Jesus said—

But Jesus said nothing.

"Answer the charges!" Caiaphas demanded.

But Jesus stood, calm and confident, and held his peace.

"I adjure you by the living God!" The high priest pounded his fist on the table. "Answer! Tell us whether you are the Christ, the Son of God!"

Looking the high priest directly in the eyes, Jesus answered, "I AM." Not a priest said a word to such an astounding claim; hissing froze on the servants' lips. "Furthermore," Jesus continued, "you shall see the Son of Man sitting at the right hand of power and coming on the clouds of heaven."

"Blasphemy!" The high priest erupted and began to rip his robes. "Blasphemy!" He swept his arms around the room. "You all heard his blasphemy. There is no need for another witness. What," he cried to the council, "is your verdict?"

"Death!" The crowd began to close in on Jesus. "We find him guilty, deserving death!"

"Death!" The high priest hit the table with finality. "So be it."

Meanwhile, Peter had been staring at the fire in the courtyard, lost in his own morbid thoughts. He had not noticed that one of the women present continued to study his face.

Finally she touched his shoulder, and he jumped.

"Forgive me," she said, "but weren't you with Jesus the Galilean, the man inside?"

Peter looked nervously around to see whether anyone else had heard her words. "No," he said. "Someone else. I have no idea what you are talking about. No." He hunched over the fire as though that were the only thing in his life right now. The sweat on his forehead glistened, though the night was chilly.

"I know I'm right," mumbled the servant woman as she left the courtyard.

In a little while Peter saw her return with three men. He didn't look up, yet he was keenly aware she was pointing at him. Suddenly the courtyard seemed crowded with enemies.

Peter leaped to his feet, shouting, "Woman! I am not with that man!"

Heads everywhere turned to look at him. An ashy dawn light dusted every face. People seemed pale but all too visible.

"Your accent, sir, is Galilean," observed one man. "You must be his disciple."

Peter, his eyes wild with fear, began to curse and to swear, "I was not! I am not! I swear it by God: I do not know the man!"

At that very instant, the rooster crowed. The door swung open, and the officers brought Jesus through the courtyard. He stumbled . . . and looked at Peter.

Peter heard the rooster crow and felt his Lord's long look like a silent dagger in his heart. He remembered the words "deny me three times." He ran from the courtyard into an alley, leaned his head against a wall, and wept bitterly.

Friday: Death on a Cross

Pilate considered the band of religious leaders gathered outside his palace—so sinfully early in the morning!—to be important enough to merit his attention. He also thought that their problem would be a minor one, briefly resolved. Therefore he strode out to meet them at a brisk pace.

"Well, let's see to it," he said, rubbing his arms against the morning chill. "What is your charge against this man?"

"Sir, he is an evildoer," announced one of the chief priests.

"Oh, well! An evildoer," said Pilate. "There are thousands

of those. You take this one and judge him according to your own laws." He bowed and turned to go in.

"Wait!" The chief priests moved forward with stern dignity. "Sir, you know that we cannot put a man to death."

"Death?" Pilate paused. "This is a matter of death?"

Pilate felt drawn to this man who carried himself so calmly in the face of such a threat. For some reason, he didn't want this Jew to die. So, after hearing the charges against Jesus, Pilate tried to avoid sentencing him to death. Time and again Pilate tried to release Jesus, but the religious leaders kept inciting the crowd against him. In desperation, Pilate even had Jesus flogged to try to satisfy the leaders. Vicious whips tore the flesh on Jesus' back, but the chief priests were not satisfied. They demanded Jesus' death, declaring that anyone who called himself a king, as Jesus had, must be an enemy of Caesar. Certainly Pilate didn't tolerate rebellion against the emperor.

Eventually the governor relented. Pilate handed Jesus into the soldiers' custody to be crucified, hung on a cross until he was dead.

Many of the crowd followed—out of Jerusalem, past the city walls, to a place called Golgotha, Aramaic for "the place of a skull."

There, at nine in the morning, they crucified him.

To the left of him they hung a robber. To the right, another robber. Jesus, the spikes through his hands and his feet, hung between.

"Father," he whispered. His lips cracked as he spoke. He swallowed. "Father," he said, "forgive them. They don't know what they're doing."

At noon the weather changed suddenly, and all creation went into mourning. Darkness descended like a pall upon the land, and only the silhouette of the Lord Christ could be discerned upon the cross. From twelve until three the sunlight failed, and in mortal isolation Jesus suffered toward his death.

Then, at three in the afternoon, Jesus arched his back, threw his body outward from the cross, raised his face to heaven, and cried, "Eli! Eli! Lama sabachthani?" which means, "My God! My God! Why have you abandoned me?"

The curious onlookers who had waited even in the darkness whispered, "Listen! He is calling for Elijah! Do you think Elijah will come to save him?"

Then they were shocked to hear him speaking straight to them out of the gloom. "I am," he groaned in a hoarse, hollow voice, "I am thirsty."

A soldier grabbed a sponge and jammed it on a reed. Then he dipped the sponge in sour wine and held up the reed so Jesus could suck on the sponge.

When Jesus had finished, the soldier stepped back but still heard him whisper, "It is finished. Father, into your hands I commend my spirit."

Jesus' head leaned sideways, but finding no pillow even upon his own shoulder, his head dropped forward to his chest. Then Jesus breathed his last and died.

At that instant, the Temple curtain was ripped in two from top to bottom. The earth trembled, rocks rolled loose, tombs tumbled open, and many of God's people who had died were raised.

The Roman officer who had given Jesus his last drink stood at the foot of the cross, looked up, and declared, "Truly, this man was the Son of God." Other soldiers, however, pierced Jesus' side with a sharp spear. They wanted to make sure he was dead.

Then a good man, a respected member of the Jewish council of elders and a seeker after God's kingdom, came to the cross. Joseph of Arimathea, having obtained permission from Pilate to take the body of the Lord, strung cords from the cross and lovingly lowered Jesus' corpse.

Several women who loved Jesus, who believed in Jesus, were watching from a distance. And when Joseph took the body to his own tomb, newly chiseled out of the rock, they followed. They watched as Jesus' battered body was wrapped in strips of linen. They saw the ledge within the tomb, the ledge where he was laid. They heard the crunch of the great stone rolled in front of the entrance.

Only then did they turn away. Only then did they leave the Lord. But even then they went to prepare spices and perfumes to anoint his body. They would return on Sunday, after the Sabbath rest.

Sunday: He's Alive!

The earth trembled at the dawn of Sunday, the first day of the week. But the three women walking to the tombs outside Jerusalem barely noticed.

Mary Magdalene, Mary the mother of James, and Salome carried their spices in delicate grief and sadness. They were going to anoint the body of the Lord before its eventual corruption and decay.

"Sisters," whispered Mary Magdalene, "who will roll the stone away for us?"

Neither of the others spoke. Neither had an answer. But the answer lay ahead of them.

When the tomb came into view, they saw that the stone had already been rolled back! The entrance stood open: dark, yawning, and—so it seemed to Mary Magdalene—empty. Nervously they began to enter. It was empty! The body was gone!

Suddenly two men dressed in white appeared. The women were terrified. "Why do you look for the living among the dead?" one of them asked. "Come, see the place where they laid him. See that he is not there. He is risen, just as he told you."

But Mary Magdalene did not go and see. She dropped her spices, grabbed her skirts, and ran back into the city without another word. She thought she knew what had happened.

"Peter!" she cried as she burst into his room. The huge disciple grabbed her and hugged her because she seemed so upset. But Mary would not be still. "Peter, they have stolen the Lord, and we do not know where they put him!"

Before she could turn around, Peter was gone from the room, racing toward the tomb. John was running with him.

Mary arrived behind them, just in time to see John go in. She could see both disciples crouching in the tomb, but she stayed at a distance, wringing her hands and trying desperately not to cry. Now and again she stamped her foot. "Gone!" she whispered. "Why would they have taken him? Why?"

Then Peter and John emerged from the tomb, blinking in the morning light and walking toward her. She ran to them with her hands on her cheeks.

"What did you see?" she whispered.

"Gone," said Peter.

Immediately Mary burst into tears. "I knew it! I knew it!" she cried.

"It's odd," Peter continued. "The burial linen is disarranged, but the cloth that was around his head is in the corner, neatly rolled. It's very odd." Then he went with John back to the city, lost in the strangeness of it all.

But Mary stayed behind, crying harder than ever before. The tears streamed down her cheeks and dropped from the end of her nose. She stumbled toward the tomb, leaned against its cold rock face, then stooped and looked in.

At the head and at the foot of the place where Jesus had lain, Mary saw two angels. "Woman," they asked, "why are you crying?"

"Because," she sobbed, "they have taken away my Lord, and I do not know where they put him."

She turned away from the darkness of the tomb and at once saw Jesus standing in the sunlight. But she did not recognize him. He was no more to her misty eyes than another man—the gardener, perhaps.

"Woman," he asked, "why are you crying? Who are you looking for?"

"Please, sir, please," she wept, "if you have carried him anywhere, just tell me, and I will take him properly away."

Then with a single word, all Life and Light and Truth became clear. The word was a common one, but it contained and conveyed a universe of love. It was her own name.

Jesus called her by name. "Mary," he said. At once her ears heard the voice that her heart knew. Her tears danced in gladness, and she laughed while she cried.

"Master, my Master!" She stretched her arms to him.

But Jesus stepped back. "Mary, do not hold on to me," he cautioned. "I have not yet returned to my Father. But go back to my friends, my disciples, and tell them that I am returning to my Father and your Father, to my God and your God."

With what lightness Mary covered the distance back to the disciples' room! With what indestructible joy she told them the message that the living Lord had given unto her. So glad was she that even their disbelief did not destroy the spirit in her, and she ran to tell the other women. These hugged her and laughed with a heavenly joy, for the women, the women were Jesus' first witnesses.

The disciples, on the other hand—impetuous Peter, gentle John, imperious James, and the others—spent most of that Sunday behind locked doors. They hid together in a single, stuffy room, fearful that the people who had killed Jesus meant also to seek and destroy them. The afternoon passed in gloom, and only when it was dark outside did one of them, Thomas, sneak away to find food.

Suddenly Jesus stood among them and said, "Peace be unto you."

They said nothing. They shrank back and stared. The face and the form were the Lord's, and the voice was familiar. But no one had rattled the bolt at the door. No one had made the hinges squeak. No one had let him in!

Slowly Jesus extended his hands to them, palms up. They saw there the wounds from the spikes...

"Jesus?"

Then he pulled back his robe, and there, in his side, was the long, serious wound from the spear.

"Lord? Master? Jesus?"

Peter let out a bark of laughter. John sank to his knees before the Lord, tears in his wide-open eyes. Others clutched their hands together, laughed, and called out his name.

"Lord, it is you!" It was Jesus and none other, Jesus and no spirit, Jesus come back from the dead, Jesus alive in the flesh!

Once again Jesus said, "Peace be unto you," for such he had promised them a lifetime ago. "You have been disciples, students of mine, these past years. Now," he said, "I make you my apostles, my messengers, for I send you out into the world even as the Father sent me into the world."

Jesus Returns to Heaven

In the days that followed, Jesus appeared to more than five hundred of his followers, but he spent most of his time with the eleven whom he had chosen. Once, when they had gathered in grateful worship before him on an appointed mountain in Galilee, Jesus said,

"All authority in heaven and on earth has been given unto me. Therefore, I myself commission you: Go out. Make disciples of all the nations. Baptize them in the name of the Father and of the Son and of the Holy Spirit. Teach them to observe everything that I have taught you. And remember, my dear ones, my laborers, remember that I am with you always, even to the end of this age."

Now, Jesus performed many other signs in the presence of his disciples, which miracles are not recorded. For if they were written down, the world itself could not contain the books of his deeds. But some were recorded that you might believe that Jesus is the Christ, the Son of the living God, and that believing, you might have life in his name.

Finally, after the risen Lord Jesus had spent forty days appearing to his people and speaking about the kingdom of God, he gathered his apostles into one place. So watchful and still was his manner that they sensed some great thing was about to occur.

"Lord," they asked, "is this the time? Will you now restore the kingdom to Israel?"

Jesus said, "It is not for you to know the times and the dates that the Father has set, so don't worry about them. Rather, you will receive power when the Holy Spirit comes upon you, and then you shall be my witnesses. Speak of me in Jerusalem, in all Judea, and in Samaria. Carry my name to all peoples, to the very end of the earth."

Then, while they were looking at him, Jesus was taken up, high, high above the dull and lumpish globe, until a cloud enveloped him and hid him from their sight.

Gone from view was Jesus. Yet the apostles continued to stare heavenward. Suddenly two men in white robes appeared and gently drew their attention back down to the earth.

"Men of Galilee," they said to the apostles, "why do you stand looking up to heaven? This Jesus, who was taken up from you, will return in the same way as you saw him go."

Slowly their eyes descended to the world below, to the reality of grassy hills, gray stone, and needy people. Slowly they walked the way to Jerusalem, there to wait for the promise of the Father.

For Jesus had promised, before his departure, "John baptized with water, but before many days you will be baptized with the Holy Spirit."

They returned to the holy city and waited.

God Creates His Church

No matter where they lived, devout Jews felt a need to travel to the holy city of Jerusalem at least once in their lives, there to celebrate before God one of the appointed religious festivals. One such festival that often drew large crowds was Pentecost, which came fifty days after Passover. At this festival loaves of bread made with yeast, the first bread baked from that year's wheat harvest, were offered to the Lord God.

So, when Jesus' followers gathered in a single place on the

morning of Pentecost, Jerusalem was crowded. All the world was represented there, and thousands witnessed the stirrings of the church at its birth. It happened in this manner.

Suddenly, without warning, a mighty sound whistled down from heaven, swept through the streets, and whirled into the house where the apostles were sitting. It was an urgent noise, like the scream of a high wind, and it filled the entire house. Then a most amazing thing took place: Above the head of each of Jesus' followers, there appeared fire in the shape of a tongue.

Then just as suddenly, all of the believers present were filled with the Holy Spirit and began to speak. They were telling everyone of God's mighty deeds. A crowd soon gathered in amazement, for the Spirit-filled believers were speaking these things in every language of every nation under heaven! The Spirit had enabled them to speak so that every person, no matter what his or her language, understood what was being said.

Some of the crowd suggested that Jesus' followers were drunk. But Peter quickly dismissed that theory. Then he courageously and carefully proclaimed to the entire crowd that Jesus—whom they had crucified and whom God had raised from the dead—was the Messiah.

"Repent," said Peter. "Be baptized every one of you in the name of Jesus Christ for the forgiveness of your sins, and you also will receive the gift of the Holy Spirit."

Because of Peter's brave stand, three thousand people believed in Jesus, were baptized in Jesus' name, and were added to Jesus' church that very day.

Peter Takes a Stand

From that day forward the apostles spoke openly of the Lord and of his resurrection. All those who believed devoted themselves joyfully to their teaching.

Willingly Jesus' followers shared with one another. Not one person went hungry or lacked for anything because those who had lands or houses sold them and gave the proceeds to those who had none. The apostles distributed goods to those in need, and no one said, "This is mine. I own it." Everything belonged to everyone.

Daily, joyfully the believers ate together in their houses, for this was the nourishment of their bodies. Then, after sharing the meal, they would share the memory of their Lord's death. Just as Jesus had instructed, they would eat the bread of Jesus' body and drink the cup of Jesus' blood.

Every day these children of their father Israel faithfully went to the Temple together, devoting themselves to prayer.

On a certain morning Peter and John were entering the Temple court by an eastern gate, on their way to pray at the appointed hour. Suddenly a man behind them set up a clamor.

The man was a beggar, for his feet and ankles had been twisted from the day of his birth. Empowered by God, Peter took the man's hand and raised him to his feet, healed! The beggar leaped and ran into the Temple, jumping and praising God. Immediately Peter began to tell people about Jesus, the one in whose name he had performed the miracle.

While Peter was still speaking, the priests, the captain of

the Temple guard, and the Sadducees surrounded him and locked both him and John in jail for the night.

"We cannot have this sort of disturbance," they explained, "or this kind of teaching. It is both foolish and dangerous—"

Dangerous indeed, for many of the people who had heard Peter believed his word, and the church had grown to about five thousand people.

In the morning all the Jewish religious leaders assembled and had Peter and John brought before them. The same Peter who had denied Jesus in a dim morning courtyard now stood face to face with Caiaphas, Annas, and the Temple authorities.

"From this moment on," they commanded, "you will neither speak, preach, nor teach in the name of Jesus. Do you understand the decree?"

Peter understood. But he would not bow before it. "Whether it is right before God to listen to you rather than to him, you judge. But regardless of what you think or even say, we will do the will of God. We have no choice but to speak of the things that we have heard and seen."

Thus Peter and all the apostles continued to talk about Jesus openly, and the church continued to grow at a phenomenal rate.

The First Martyr

Because of the growing numbers of believers, the disciples appointed leaders to help take care of the people. One such man was named Stephen, a bold and eloquent witness for Jesus. The elders of the Jewish council didn't like what Stephen had to say, so they arrested him and had false witnesses accuse him of a capital crime, of blasphemy.

Stephen's defense before the council was simple but effective. He spoke of Israel's history—of Abraham, Isaac, and Jacob; of Moses; of David; and of Solomon. He reminded them that their ancestors had always killed God's prophets. Then he announced that they were just like their ancestors, for they had murdered Jesus, God's Messiah.

Stephen's accusation infuriated the elders to the extent that they dragged him outside the city and began stoning him. The false witnesses, after laying their robes at the feet of a man named Saul, added their stones to the deadly barrage. But not even death could shake Stephen's faith, so as he fell dying, he prayed, as Jesus had earlier, "Lord, hold not this sin against them."

In that same day opposition to the young church changed from merely hard words to hard action. Many people—the man named Saul in particular—persecuted the believers. Saul entered their houses, dragged off men and women alike, and committed them to prison.

So frightening was the uproar in Jerusalem that many believers fled the city and scattered throughout the regions of Judea and Samaria.

Sad was the motive that moved them out, but the result was joyous, for they took with them the name of Jesus and everywhere preached good news about the kingdom of God and his Christ.

Now Saul's fiery desire to destroy the church could not be contained within the little city of Jerusalem. He was so fanatically zealous for the old traditions that he vowed to obliterate the name of Jesus wherever it might be found. So he obtained the legal right to round up believers even in Damascus in Syria, to tie them up, and to bring them back to Jerusalem.

Papers in hand, Saul and his men journeyed northward, nothing hindering the threat and the havoc he intended.

But just outside Damascus, a mighty light blazed all around him and blasted him to the ground. Then he heard a voice asking, "Saul! Saul! Why are you persecuting me?"

The proud persecutor, the defender of the faith, was stunned by the bright divinity and mumbled, "Who? Who are you, Lord?"

"I am Jesus," replied the voice, "the one you are persecuting!"

The men with Saul stood speechless, hearing a voice but seeing no one and understanding not a word.

"Stand up!" Jesus ordered. "I hereby appoint you to be my representative, to tell foreigners and pagans about me. Open their eyes. Turn them from the darkness to light. Turn them from Satan to God, so they may receive forgiveness of sins and a place among God's people."

Saul tried to stand and immediately stumbled. He was totally blind! So his companions helped him up and then led him by the hand to Damascus.

For three days Paul sat in a Damascan room, in a house on a street called Straight, neither eating nor drinking nor seeing—only praying. Then, with hesitation, but under pressure from the Lord, a believer named Ananias came to him.

"Saul?" he asked.

"Yes," said the blind man quietly.

"Brother Saul?"

"Yes! Yes!" Saul raised his sightless face hopefully. He had been called brother.

"Jesus, the Just One, has sent me that you might regain your sight and be filled with the Holy Spirit. Thus!" Ananias laid his hands on the trembling head. Immediately something like scales fell from Saul's eyes. He could see! Then he wasted no time in explanations or in discourse but rose and was baptized.

For the next several days, Saul went with other believers to the Jewish synagogues. These had been his original destination, but now his purposes had changed. Instead of arresting people, he told everyone that Jesus was the Son of God. Every day he entered into debate with his fellow Jews, proving with powerful arguments that Jesus was the Christ.

Good News to All People

From the very beginning, the young church had preached Jesus as Christ to those who had long awaited the coming of Christ, to the Jews, for it was unto the family of Israel that God had promised the Messiah.

But what of those who, for centuries, had not been the chosen people of God? What about the Gentiles—the Greeks, the Romans, the Egyptians, all the other non-Jewish peoples? Could they believe in Jesus, become a part of his church? Should the apostles proclaim that Jesus had come to save all peoples and not just the Jewish people?

On the coast of the Mediterranean Sea, in Caesarea, there was stationed a cohort of Roman soldiers commanded by a man named Cornelius. He, too, was a Roman, a Gentile. Yet he feared God, gave freely to the poor, and prayed devoutly, constantly to the Lord God of Israel.

One day while he was praying, he was terrified to see an angel of God enter the room and stand before him.

"Cornelius," said the angel.

Shrinking backward, Cornelius replied, "What, Lord?"

"Your prayers and gifts to the poor have ascended to God," the angel said. "Now send messengers to Joppa and have them bring back one Simon who is called Peter."

Indeed, Simon was then in Joppa with people whom Philip had called unto Christ. His presence in that town was no secret, for he had raised to life Tabitha, a woman loved by one and all. People knew where to find one so full of the Spirit as Peter.

On the day after Cornelius's vision, Peter had gone to the roof of his house. He wanted someplace quiet to pray. After a while, he became extremely hungry. But before his food could be prepared, he fell into a trance.

His eyes looked upward, and he saw heaven open wide. Then down from heaven floated a strange container; something that looked like a huge sheet gathered at its four corners descended to the earth. Within the sheet Peter saw all kinds of animals, reptiles, and birds. Then he heard a voice command him: "Rise, Peter. Kill and eat."

Peter was shocked at the mistake. "No, Lord!" said Peter

the ever abrupt. "Oh, no!" said Peter, impulsive apostle, so certain of himself. "I obey the law of Moses. I never eat anything judged to be impure or unclean..."

"Do not call anything impure," the voice returned, "that God has declared clean!"

Twice more the voice invited Simon Peter to eat. Twice more the stubborn apostle refused to touch an unclean beast. Then the sheet was snatched back into heaven, and Peter heard a knock at the door below.

He was perplexed, wondering what this vision could mean, when the Spirit said to him, "Peter, three men are looking for you. Go down to them. Then go most willingly away with them, for I have sent them."

Immediately Peter descended to meet them. "I am the one you are looking for," he informed them. "What do you want?"

"Well, we are from Cornelius, a centurion in Caesarea," they began, "a good and God-fearing person..."

"A Roman! A Gentile! The unclean!" thought Peter.

"He received direction from a holy angel to send for you that he might hear in his own house what you have to say..."

"Go with them willingly," the Spirit had said.

"Will you come with us?" they asked.

Sometimes Peter spoke so loudly that he practically bellowed in all his certainty. But whenever Peter discovered what a fool he had been to bellow in the first place, he spoke softly, lowly. So he answered their request with three low, humble words: "I will go."

When Peter came to Caesarea and entered the house of

the centurion, Cornelius bowed down at his feet and worshiped him. But Peter lifted him up. "Stand," he said, still in
lowly voice. "I am as human as you are."

Then he looked around and saw many people gathered to
meet him. Gentiles! Gentiles, every one of them!

"You know how we Jews hesitated to preach the word of
God to Gentiles," he said, "but God has shown me that I
should call no one unclean or impure. Truly," and now his
voice began to rise, for it was of the Lord he intended to
speak, "truly, I perceive that God shows favoritism to no one.
He lifts no single person or people above the others. But in
every nation and in every ethnic group, everyone who fears
him and believes in Jesus is acceptable to him!"

Then Peter opened his mouth and began to tell the people all about Christ—his life, his death, his resurrection. With
these words were the hearts of the Gentiles filled, and with
more, for the Holy Spirit came on them. They then did just
what the Jewish believers had done on Pentecost. They spoke
in tongues, praising God.

"If God gives them what he gave us when we believed,"
thought Peter in amazement, "who am I to oppose God? So he
ordered, "Bring water!" Then he baptized the Gentiles in the
name of Jesus Christ! The church would never be the same.

The Church Triumphant

In those days a new King Herod ruled Judea, Galilee, and
the surrounding area. He was neither the Herod of Jesus'

birth—Herod the Great—nor the Herod of Jesus' death—
Herod Antipas. He was Herod Agrippa I, grandson of the former and nephew of the latter. Just like his predecessors, he
caused anguish for Christ and his people.

Herod commanded that the most important apostle of the
young church be arrested. So it was that Simon Peter was seized
and held in prison under the guard of four squads of soldiers.
There he would remain, supposed Herod, until the Passover celebration was over and he could bring the troublemaker to trial.

But God had a different idea. The very night before
Herod meant to execute Peter publicly, an angel freed Peter
from his chains and led him to safety through the open gates
of the prison. Thus Peter's life was saved, and his preaching of
the good news of Jesus continued unabated.

When Christ met him on the road to Damascus, Saul,
who was also called Paul, stopped persecuting the church of
Christ and started proclaiming the gospel of Christ. During
the years following his conversion, Paul devoted himself to
telling as many people as he could about Jesus.

Christians in the Syrian city of Antioch—for believers
were first called Christians in Antioch—recognized the goodness and force of Paul's preaching. So, at the prompting of the
Holy Spirit, they commissioned Paul and Barnabas to carry
the good news of Jesus westward.

Therefore, Paul, a Jew by birth and a Roman citizen; Paul,
a Pharisee by training and a Christian by the grace of God;
Paul, an apostle and a preacher of the good news of Christ

took the word to Asia Minor, to Macedonia, to Greece, and even to the end of the earth.

Throughout his life and ministry, Paul suffered hardships and faced many persecutions. He was imprisoned on numerous occasions, shipwrecked three times, and once stoned and left for dead. Yet he always remained true to the One who had confronted him on the road to Damascus. He told people everywhere about Jesus. He started churches and wrote many letters (some of which are included in the Bible) to the people in those churches. In his letters, he encouraged and instructed believers, helping them to think and live as Christians should. Thus Paul's own faith became an example for all believers.

As Paul faced the end of his life, he was not afraid to speak of death. He had lived well, and he was ready to die. Therefore, it was with a peaceful soul that the apostle warned his friend Timothy of the hard times to come. Shortly before he died, he wrote,

"Paul, an apostle of Christ Jesus by God's will, to Timothy, my beloved child. May you receive grace, mercy, and peace from God the Father and Christ Jesus our Lord!

"In the presence of God and of Christ Jesus, I charge you to preach the Word. Be persistent whether the times are favorable or unfavorable. Convince, reprimand, and encourage God's people. Show the utmost patience in your teaching.

"For the time is coming when people will not accept sound teaching. Rather, they will gather teachers who meet their own likings, who scratch their ears by telling them what they want to hear. They will turn away from the truth and wander into myths. But you, Timothy, remain steady. Endure suffering and the persecutions that are to come. Do the work of an evangelist and thus fulfill your ministry.

"For I am already on the point of being sacrificed; the time of my departure has come. I have fought the good fight. I have finished the race. I have kept the faith. For this reason, there is waiting for me the crown of righteousness, which the Lord, the Righteous Judge, will award to me as well as to everyone who looks for his return."

A Call to Endure

As the church increased in size and strength, opposition to the church increased in frequency and intensity. Thus, in the course of time, it became dangerous for someone to proclaim faith in Jesus Christ, dangerous because such witness endangered not only one's freedom but also one's life. So the leaders of the church encouraged the disciples with strong words uttered in holy conviction.

Many who heard these words died most wretched deaths within the persecution. But the faith for which they died did not die, and the words that made death, even death, a joyful opportunity to serve the Lord—these words continue still.

"You are not alone in the struggle. You are surrounded by a great cloud of witnesses who by their faith did not shrink back but rather performed the tasks to which God had called them. Remember them.

"Remember Abraham, called out to a foreign land; Sarah, able in her old age to conceive a son; Isaac, who was that son; his son Jacob, and Jacob's son, Joseph. All of these were given a promise by God but died before the promise was fulfilled. Because of their faith the promise was real unto them. By their faith they lived between the giving and the keeping of the promise.

"Remember Moses and Israel, who by faith crossed the Red Sea as if on dry ground. Remember Gideon and Samson, Samuel, David, and the prophets!

"Remember those who were mighty in war, and those also who were tortured, mocked, beaten, and imprisoned.

"Remember all these and know that you are not alone! These faithful go before you and surround you, for you have received the promise they were looking for! You have received Jesus. Therefore, lay aside every weight, every sin that clings so closely. Run with perseverance the race God has set before you.

"Most of all, most of all, remember Jesus, the pioneer and the perfecter of our faith; Jesus, who is the promise perfectly fulfilled; Jesus, who endured the cross and is seated at the right hand of God's throne. Remember him, when you grow weary. Remember Jesus."

The Final Chapter

Every story, whether human or divine, must have a beginning and an ending. This story, God's story, began when God created all that exists. It will end in the future when God re-creates and remakes heaven and earth. John—brother of James, companion of Peter, the disciple whom Jesus loved—recorded the end to God's story in the last book of the Bible, the book of Revelation.

"I, John, your brother, share with you in Jesus the persecution and the kingdom and the patient endurance, for I was exiled to the tiny island called Patmos on account of my testimony of Jesus. In that place I was given visions of things that are to come.

"I was in the Spirit one Sunday, when I saw a throne and one seated upon the throne, one finer and more brilliant than jasper and carnelian. Twenty-four elders, wearing crowns and clothed in white garments, surrounded the throne. On its four sides were four living creatures: the first like a lion, the second like an ox, the third with the face of a man, and the fourth a flying eagle. Day and night, never ceasing, they sing, 'Holy, holy, holy is the Lord God Almighty, who was and is and is to come!' The twenty-four elders bow down before him who sits on the throne and worship him who lives forevermore.

"I noticed that the one on the throne held a scroll sealed with seven seals. Then an angel cried, 'Who is worthy to break the seals and open the scroll?'

"But neither in heaven, nor on the earth, nor under the earth was anyone found worthy, so I wept because there was no one worthy to open the scroll or to look inside. But one of the elders said, 'Don't cry. There is one who is worthy.'

"Then I saw a Lamb that looked as though it had been

slain, yet it was standing! The Lamb took the scroll from the one on the throne, and the elders and the creatures sang, 'You are worthy to take the scroll, for you were killed and with your blood provided forgiveness of sins. You ransomed people for God from every tribe, tongue, and nation. You have made them priests to God, and they shall reign on earth!'

"When Jesus, the Lamb, opened the seven seals of the scroll, God's final judgment was pronounced and carried out upon his sinful and rebellious earth. Then, when all was done and wars had ceased and God had taken to himself his victory—for Satan and Death were held captive in the lake of fire—I saw a new heaven and a new earth, for the first heaven and the first earth had been destroyed.

"Moreover, I saw the holy city, the new Jerusalem, coming down from heaven, prepared as a bride made lovely for her husband. Then I heard a booming voice from the throne saying: 'Listen, the dwelling place of God is now with humans. He will dwell with them, and they shall be his people! God himself will wipe the tears from every eye, and death shall be no more. There will be neither mourning nor crying nor pain, for the former things have passed away.'

"Then he who sits on the throne said, 'Behold, I make all things new! I AM the Alpha and the Omega, the Beginning and the End. To the thirsty I will freely give water from the spring of the water of life. To those who endure I will give this heritage. I will be their God and they shall be my people.'

"Then Jesus, the Lamb, said, 'Surely, I am coming soon.'

"Amen! So be it! Come quickly, Lord Jesus!"

FOR FURTHER READING